easy woodcarving

by Cyndi Joslyn

FOX CHAPEL
PUBLISHING

Dedication

To Jenna, the light of my life and my continuing source of inspiration.

Thanks to:

Joyce Jacobson for sharing her stuff with me
Les Ramsay for sharing his great carving wisdom with me

© 2006 by Fox Chapel Publishing Company, Inc.

Easy Woodcarving is an original work, first published in 2006 by Fox Chapel Publishing Company, Inc. The patterns contained herein are copyrighted by the author. Readers may make three copies of these patterns for personal use. The patterns themselves, however, are not to be duplicated for resale or distribution under any circumstances. Any such copying is a violation of copyright law.

ISBN 978-1-56523-288-4

Publisher's Cataloging-in-Publication Data

Joslyn-Carhart, Cyndi.

Easy woodcarving / by Cyndi Joslyn. -- East Petersburg, PA : Fox Chapel Publishing, c2006.

p. ; cm.

ISBN 978-1-56523-288-4

1. Wood-carving--Handbooks, manuals, etc. 2. Wood-carving--Technique. 3. Wood-carving--Patterns. 4. Folk art--Patterns.
I. Title.

TT199.7 .J67 2006
736/.4--dc22   0609

To learn more about the other great books from
Fox Chapel Publishing, or to find a retailer near you,
call toll-free 800-457-9112 or visit us at *www.FoxChapelPublishing.com*.

Note to Authors: We are always looking for talented
authors to write new books in our area of woodworking, design,
and related crafts. Please send a brief letter describing your idea to
Acquisition Editor, 1970 Broad Street, East Petersburg, PA 17520.

Printed in China
First printing: September 2006
Second printing: October 2007
Third printing: July 2009

about the author

Cyndi Joslyn is a professional woodcarver with a flare for handcarved folk art figures. Her work is sold through several exclusive shops and galleries across the country. She has also designed and carved more than two dozen ornaments and figurines for Big Sky Carvers, a Montana company that produces and distributes resin-cast ornaments of her original handcarved designs.

In the 1990s, Cyndi took part in a volunteer effort to produce one of the first handcarved carousels created since the 1930s. This collection of 38 carved ponies and two chariots, completed in 1995 in Missoula, Montana, drew national attention. Her outstanding talent earned Cyndi the distinction of being the only woman "head carver" on the project.

As an author, Cyndi's articles have appeared in *Wood Carving Illustrated* and *Woodworking for Women*. She has also authored two books: *North Woods Nativity*, featuring step-by-step directions on how to carve a sixteen-piece woodland nativity set, and *Carving Santas from Around the World*, an easy-to-understand handbook that guides beginners through fifteen Santa carvings based on figures from around the globe. *Easy Woodcarving* is her most recent book from Fox Chapel Publishing.

A woodcarving teacher for the past 14 years, Cyndi loves to share her passion with others. She works tirelessly to perpetuate the art by encouraging beginners and helping to instill in them a love of carving.

To learn more about Cyndi, visit her website at *www.cyndijoslyn.com* where you can view and purchase her work and sign up for her e-mail woodcarving newsletter.

contents

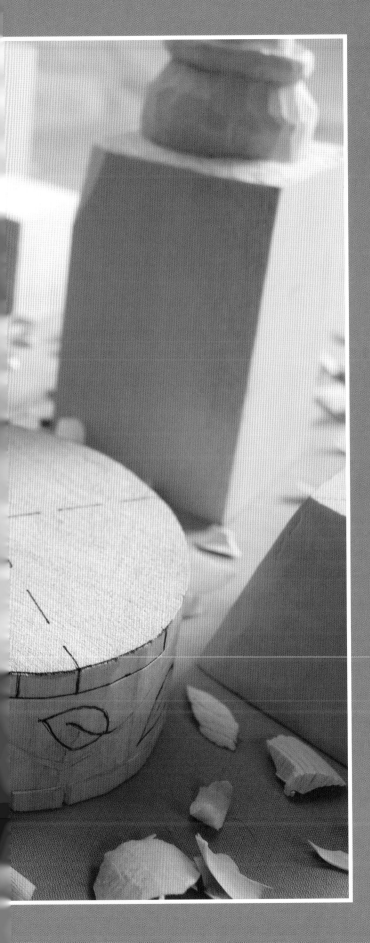

introduction

Starting anything new—whether it is learning a new job, a new project, or a new skill—can often be intimidating. When I first started carving, I didn't even know how to find wood—that is how little I knew about the craft. I felt intimidated by the whole process. I wanted to carve, but I had a list of questions that kept me from trying: How do I find wood? What kind of wood do I use? What about knives? Do I really need to resharpen them before I use them? How do other tools, like gouges and chisels, fit into the picture? And how do I apply one of these patterns to the wood?

I answered those questions on my own with a lot of wasted time, a few almost unsalvageable projects, and a lot of frustration. But carving doesn't have to be like that! Regardless of your age or level of experience, carving can be a truly satisfying process.

The purpose of this book is to answer those questions, to dispel any feelings of frustration that beginners may encounter, and to help beginners become enthusiastic about carving and discover what a soul-inspiring and enriching craft it can be. Rather than frustrate you with unnecessary complications and structure, I will guide you through the beginning stages and help you discover your own originality and creativity.

If you have ever read any books on carving, you probably noticed that they are full of traditional techniques, which (while they work) can be confusing or difficult for the beginner. The projects found in many pattern books deviate very little from a small group of subjects.

With this book, I aim to shake up the carving world by presenting a more contemporary approach. From an instructor's standpoint, I want to provide you with a place to start and then let you take your own creativity and move to whatever level you feel comfortable exploring. To that

end, a lot of my carving techniques come from what I call "block carving." That is, you start with a block of wood and you carve it into something. This method allows beginning carvers more opportunities to be creative, rather than starting off with something that is already pre-shaped to conform to someone else's idea of how it should look. To provide you with the best starting point, I have included the following items:

- easy-to-use patterns that more closely resemble the patterns that crafters use instead of the traditional patterns that show an outline of the finished carving
- techniques for carving basic shapes, like cylinders and cubes
- step-by-step sequences on how to move from those basic shapes to a finished three-dimensional project
- simple painting and finishing instructions in an easy-to-read format that will help your carving last a lifetime

In short, this book offers the beginning carver a strong foundation that includes how to use and care for the basic tools, the pros and cons of the different types of woods, general carving information, basic techniques, guidelines and safety instructions, wood finishing, pattern making, and some unconventional carving projects, which are inspired by the growing interest in home décor using handmade and folk art items. All of this is offered with step-by-step patterns, charts, and other visual materials to make the carving experience easier to understand. Above all, however, this book is meant to inspire, instill confidence, and help beginning carvers of all ages and walks of life discover the joy of carving.

—Cyndi Joslyn

getting started

The place to begin carving for the very first time is not with your first cut into the wood. You actually begin carving when you gather the tools you will need to make your first project. Some carvers skip over this beginning step completely. That path may seem like the quickest way to complete your piece, but what it ultimately does is put you even farther behind.

By learning about the different tools available to carvers—and there's more than just a knife!—you are actually filing away information that will make your carving experience more enjoyable. As you'll learn in this chapter, different tools perform different functions. Knowing which tool to use when and how to handle each one will make you a better carver. You'll also learn that sharp tools are essential. Many beginning carvers quit shortly after they begin because they find the act of removing wood to be so difficult. Often, that difficulty is the result of a dull knife, and it's something that can be overcome by learning a bit about sharpening.

Safety equipment is just as important as tools, and we'll cover these items, too. Carving in a safe environment and protecting yourself from injury is an all-important part of learning to enjoy carving.

I'll also present some information on selecting wood and using finishes. The more information you can gather about this art form before you start, the easier your first cut will be. Let's get started!

setting up your work space

It doesn't take a huge shop and thousands of dollars of equipment to begin a very satisfying experience in woodcarving. You don't even need a space where you can permanently set up shop, so to speak. The kitchen table or space in an existing craft room is an adequate carving space for beginning carvers. Just make sure you have a work surface of about 18" x 32".

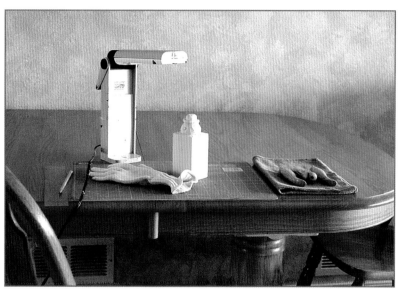

Permanent space is not necessary. A little room at the kitchen table is all the space you need to set up shop.

Basic carving space. This is my carving space. I find that wire shelves and movable storage drawers hold all of my supplies conveniently within arm's reach.

You'll also need a place to store your tools and projects when you are not carving. All of your tools, equipment, supplies, and wood should easily fit in a large plastic container. A shop vacuum, stored in a corner or under a table, makes cleanup a breeze.

lighting

Good lighting is very important. You must be able to clearly see the wood and where you are cutting without shadows. I use a full-spectrum, non-glare natural light, such as an Ott-Lite, which is commonly used by quilters and crafters. A full-spectrum light allows me to see in greater detail. The one in the photos is a compact version that can be folded up for storage if desired.

self-healing mat

If you are carving on a kitchen or dining room table, a self-healing mat, like the Olfa one pictured in the top left photo, provides plenty of protection for your tabletop in case of an occasional slip. Olfa does make a translucent 3 mm mat that is twice as thick as their standard green mat and is specifically designed for use with heavy-duty cutters and craft knives.

seating

Another item to consider, especially if you do a lot of carving, is a comfortable chair. I experimented with several before I found one I really liked. I use an ergonomic office chair with a variety of adjustments for height, lumbar support, etc. Although this certainly is not a required item, if you find yourself doing a lot of carving, it is something your body will truly appreciate.

understanding basic carving tools

There are literally hundreds of carving tools with very specific purposes. But I have learned that working with so many tools can be difficult and time consuming. You spend a lot of time trying to locate one particular tool and then even more time just moving from one tool to another. From a production standpoint, this is not very efficient. It can also get quite expensive.

As far as I am concerned, the more you can get done with one tool, the better off you are going to be. I have 35 to 45 different tools right now, but the ones I use over and over again are those I selected as the five basic tools: a bench knife, a detail knife, a #3 16 mm (⅝") gouge or a #3 22 mm (⅞") gouge, a skew knife, and a 1 mm V-tool. These five tools will prove to be the mainstays for most of your carving pursuits.

Before you go out and buy any tools, take a look at the following information about the different types of carving tools. Understanding the basic types and their functions will allow you customize your tool set to suit the kinds of projects that you prefer.

One word of caution: Though it may be enticing, resist the urge to buy inexpensive sets of carving tools. They are likely to chip and break more easily and need to be replaced more often, whereas a few well-selected, quality carving tools that are well maintained will serve you for years. Quality tools stay sharper longer, and sharp tools are the foundation of a comfortable, quality carving experience. I have tools that I've been using every day for fifteen years, and they are still in good shape. Good tools are lifelong carving companions, so do not skimp on quality.

Due to the increasing popularity of hand carving, tools and supplies for this art form are more readily available today through quality craft stores, mail-order companies, and the Internet. In fact, I buy most of what I need online where I can research and study each product. You can learn about tools by using the following tool section and by using online resources to make more educated decisions about which tools are right for you.

knives

Knives are used to score wood, to round and shape, and to carve and clean up details. Any carving knives should have comfortable handles and blades that are made of hardened and tempered high-carbon steel. Look for tools that have been honed by the manufacturer. Honing means that the tools have been factory sharpened and polished and are ready to use.

Knives are generally identified by type, and each type of knife varies in its characteristics depending on the manufacturer. Regardless of the type of knife you are using, knives with blades that are 1½ inches long and under are good choices for the beginning carver. Anything longer than 1½ inches can be intimidating and harder to control.

To hold a knife, place the handle of the knife in the palm of your hand with the blade going in the same direction as your thumb, and then wrap all four fingers around the handle. This is called an overhand grip. Your thumb provides the pushing action against the back of the blade or helps to hold the wood in place.

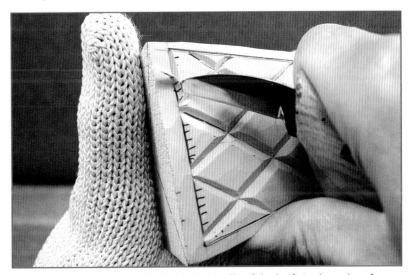

Overhand grip with a knife. Hold the handle of the knife in the palm of your hand. The blade goes the same direction as your thumb, and all four fingers should wrap around the handle.

knives you should know

Here, we will take a brief look at some of the common types of knives. We'll be using all of these to complete the projects in this book.

Bench knife. The bench knife has a sturdy blade and is used for preliminary rounding and shaping.

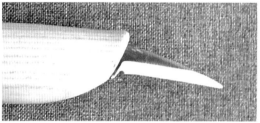

Detail knife. Delicate details are carved with the thin, sharp-tipped blade of a detail knife.

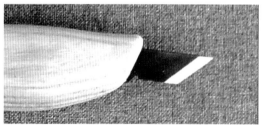

Skew knife. The 45-degree angle of this knife blade creates the geometric shapes associated with chip carving.

bench knife: A bench knife is the foundation knife of your tool collection. It generally has a wider blade than most other types of knives. Because of its sturdy blade, a good amount of pressure can be applied to deeply score wood with this knife. It can also be used for rounding and for some preliminary shaping.

detail knife: This tool is perfect for getting into areas that are too small to access with a bench knife because it has a much thinner blade that comes to a very fine point. It is used to remove wood in tight areas and to carve delicate details. The tip of this knife is very thin, so extra care must be taken when carving with it. Too much pressure and the tip will break off.

skew knife: This is a specialty knife used to create the wonderful triangular-shaped cuts that denote chip carvings, which entail cutting a series of freeform or geometric patterns on flat pieces of wood. The skew knife has a short, flat edge that is honed to a 45-degree angle to create the accent wedge of the chip-carved triangle. This knife is also called the "stabbing knife."

The skew knife can be held with an overhand grip (like a dagger) or with an underhand grip, just like you would hold a pencil.

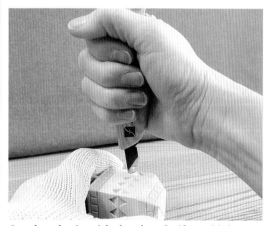

Overhand grip with the skew knife. Hold the skew knife just as you would hold a dagger.

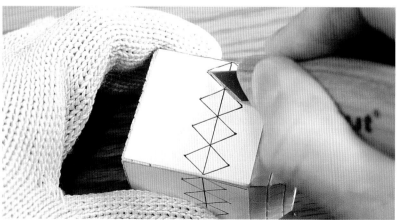

Underhand grip with the skew knife. To use the underhand grip, hold the skew knife as you would hold a pencil. While this grip and use of the skew knife is a little untraditional, I have found it to be the most effective method for beginning chip carvings.

gouges

Gouges are shaped pieces of sharpened metal that are attached to wooden handles. Typically, a gouge has only one beveled edge. They are used to shape wooden surfaces and create texture in carvings. Gouges are identified by the size, or width, of the blade, the curvature of the blade, and the style of the tool.

The degree of curvature in a gouge is known as the "sweep." The sweep of a gouge is identified by a number. Each manufacturer has its own system for classifying the degree of this curvature. In general, a low sweep number indicates a shallow curve and a higher number indicates a deeper curve. The deeper curved tools remove more wood and are good for roughing out. The deeper the curve, the more texture is created in the wood.

Another consideration in gouge selection is blade length. Blade length determines how many times a gouge can be sharpened. Each time a tool is sharpened, a tiny portion of its metal edge is ground away. A blade length of 2 to 4 inches can be sharpened significantly more times than a gouge whose tempered end is only ½ inch.

To hold a gouge, place the handle of the gouge across the palm of your hand with the blade pointing away from your thumb; then, wrap all four fingers around the handle, and close your thumb on top of your fingers, almost as if you were holding an ice pick. Of course, you'll be using a controlled cutting motion, not a quick stabbing motion when you are carving!

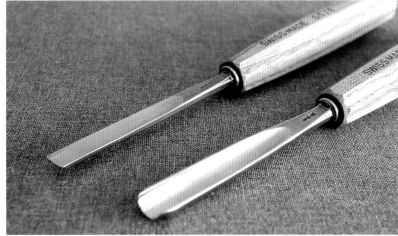

Sweep. The tool on the left is a gouge with a #5 sweep, whereas the tool on the right is a #9. The sweep indicates the curvature of the blade.

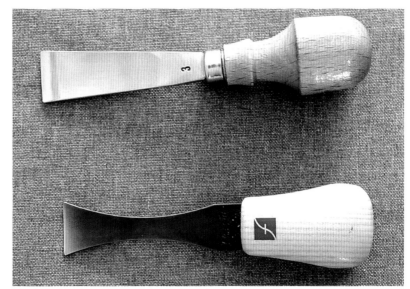

Blade length. The price of the tool on the top is almost twice that of the tool on the bottom. However, its functional life is many times greater because of the length of its blade, which makes it a very good value—even at a higher price.

Grip. To hold a gouge, place the handle across the palm of your hand and wrap all four fingers around the handle, closing your thumb on top of your fingers.

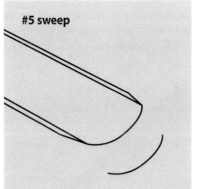

#5 sweep

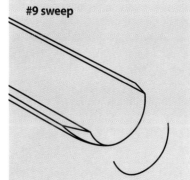

#9 sweep

Sweep and texture. The sweep of a gouge determines the texture it leaves in wood. Higher-numbered gouges remove more wood and create deeper texture.

common gouge blade sizes and sweeps

Most gouges of any given sweep come in a variety of blade sizes. For example, a gouge with a #3 sweep might be available in blades that are anywhere from 6 mm to 20 mm wide. We'll look at a few different gouges, focusing mostly on sweep, since it is the sweep that primarily determines the shape of the tool. I will also say a few words about blade width.

gouges: Your normal gouge is any gouge with a sweep between #1 and #11. These tools have anywhere from no curve to an extreme U-shaped blade. Gouges come in a variety of blade widths ranging from .5 to 60 mm.

The #3 16 mm (⅝") gouge or #3 22 mm (⅞") gouge that I recommended as basic tools are gouges with only a slight sweep, so they will remove smaller amounts of wood, making them easy to manage for a beginner. I have found this tool size range to be very versatile—not too large for a small handheld project but still quite effective when roughing out a 22"-tall Santa.

chisels and skews: Chisels and skews are gouges that have no sweep. They are completely flat at the cutting edge, but a chisel's edge is straight and a skew's edge is angled, or skewed. Chisels work well to outline projects, such as the *Welcome Sign* on page 130. Skews are handy for getting into tight angled places,

Chisel and skew. The gouge with the flat head is called a chisel (left). A flat chisel with an angled edge is called a skew (not to be confused with the skew knife).

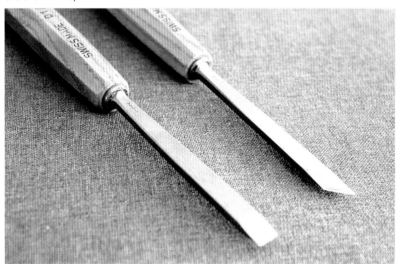

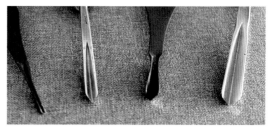

V-tools. V-tools form a V-shaped trench and are especially useful for creating fur and hair.

such as the place where Santa's mustache intersects his beard in the project on page 118. Chisels are also referred to as #1 sweep. I hold the skew as I would any other gouge.

V-tools: A V-tool is a useful specialty gouge. Its sweep is in the shape of a V, and its function is to carve an angled trench with straight sides and a V-shaped bottom edge in one carved stroke. V-tools are very handy for carving outlines and cleaning up edges of recessed wood and are also used to create a variety of textures—from crosshatching and scrollwork to creating the textures of fur and hair. Larger V-tools can be used with a mallet.

V-tools are a little more complicated when it comes to deciphering their descriptions. Some manufacturers describe their tools in degrees, such as 45, 60, and 90 degrees. A 45-degree V-tool will give you a narrower trench, and the trench will appear darker in color. A 90-degree V-tool will give you a wider trench that will appear lighter in color. Swiss tools use numbers to designate their degree of angle. For example, #15 is 45 degrees, #12 is 60 degrees, and #13 is 90 degrees.

A V-tool can be held like a knife or like a gouge, depending on the area you want to carve. The 1 mm V-tool in this book is used to create fine lines and details. It could also be used to create the texture of fur or hair.

common gouge styles

In addition to their designations by blade size and sweep, gouges can also be broken down by style. Differences in handles, overall size, and intended use define the categories.

traditional tools: Traditional carving gouges are 9½ to 11 inches long with blade lengths of 3½ to 4 inches. They have octagonal wooden handles from ¾ to 1 inch in diameter. Traditional tools are also available in widths up to 60 millimeters. These tools, especially the larger widths, are frequently used with the aid of a carving mallet.

palm tools: Palm tools are gouges with shorter, rounded handles that are specially designed to conform to the inside curvature of your palm. Rather than being tapped with a mallet, palm tools are powered by direct pressure from the hand.

intermediate tools: Intermediate tools are gouges that are approximately 8 inches in length with blades that range from 2 to 2¼ inches. The handles are ⅝ inches in diameter. These versatile tools can be used with or without a mallet.

mallets

A mallet is used to tap a gouge or chisel into the wood. There are several different styles. Some are flat-faced squares or rectangles, but the turned mallet is the one most often associated with carving. A turned mallet has a smooth, round surface that evenly impacts the handle of the tool regardless of what part of the mallet strikes the handle. This feature makes the turned mallet good for a beginning woodcarver.

Mallets come in different weights, usually 12 ounces to 36 ounces. Lighter mallets are used with small-diameter gouges; heavier mallets are used with larger carving tools. It is the weight of the mallet, not the arm swing behind it that drives the gouge through the wood.

Mallets are tapped not swung. Never use steel hammers on your gouges because they will quickly damage the handles. I prefer the newer high-tech version of the turned mallet with a urethane head because they are quieter with less vibration and are gentler on the tool handles.

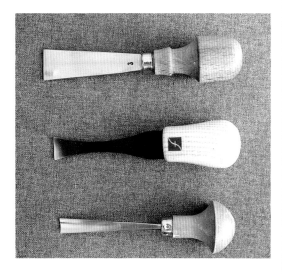

Palm tools. Palm tools are about 4½" long with handles that fit the inside surface of your hand.

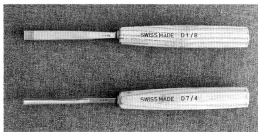

Intermediate tools. Intermediate tools can be used with or without a mallet.

Mallet use. This photo shows how to properly hold a mallet. A 12 to 18 ounce mallet is a good choice for a beginning carver.

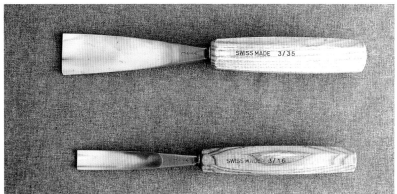

Wide blades. Gouges with wide blades are commonly used with a mallet.

choosing your first tools

The first five tools on this chart are the mainstays of any carver's toolbox. With them, you can complete any project in this book. The other tools on this list are good additions to your basic toolbox. Each of these tools performs a specific function. That function can be done with one of the five mainstay tools, but these extra tools are specially made to accomplish a certain task.

My recommendation is that you start with the five mainstays. Buy the best tools you can with the money you have to spend on your hobby. As your skills and interest in carving grow, purchase the other tools on this list.

five basic tools

Tool photo	What it is	Why you need it	Where you use it
	Bench knife	To score wood and round preliminary shapes	
	Detail knife	To carve in tight areas where a bench knife won't reach and carve details	
	#3 ⅝" (16 mm) gouge (shallow sweep)*	To rough out preliminary shapes	
	1 mm V-tool	To incise fine lines	
	Skew knife	To make geometric chip carving cuts	

* The #3 ⅝" gouge and the #3 ⅞" gouge are interchangeable. For the beginning carver, only one is required.

additional tools

Tool photo	What it is	Why you need it	Where you use it
	#3 ⅞" (22 mm) gouge (shallow sweep)	To remove large amounts of wood and rough out preliminary shapes	
	#7 4 mm (³⁄₁₆") gouge (medium sweep)	To add texture	
	#7 14 mm (½") gouge	To create large, deep recessed areas (may be used with mallet)	
	#5 3 mm (⅛") gouge (medium sweep)	To remove wood and add texture in small areas	

sharpening tools

You should no more carve with a dull tool than you would shave with a dull razor. In both cases, the result will be much the same—nicks and scrapes. The sharper and more highly polished the surface of the knife, the more easily it slides through the wood. Once a blade gets dull, you need to use more force to push it through the wood, and the knife catches and snags.

If you choose to sharpen your tools yourself, I suggest you invest in the proper equipment and a good book on how to sharpen tools. Because tool sharpening is an art unto itself and entire books have been written just on sharpening, I will not be covering that process here. Sharpening requires patience and practice, and you may go through many good tools before you perfect it.

If you choose not to sharpen your own tools, an option I highly recommend for beginners is to find someone in your area who can do it for you. Make sure to look for someone who has experience in sharpening *carving* tools. Many carving clubs have someone who really enjoys the art of tool sharpening, and, for a very minimal price, they can keep your tools in tiptop shape. Woodworking stores are also a good resource for finding people who sharpen tools.

strops

Even if you decide not to sharpen your tools yourself, you will want to have the tools necessary to strop all of your blades. Stropping, or honing, is a process used to regularly polish a tool's edge. The goal of stropping is to maintain the sharpness of the tool and postpone the actual sharpening process for as long as possible because, each time you sharpen a tool, you grind away a portion of its metal edge, thus reducing its lifespan.

If you do not strop your tools, you will start knocking the points off knives and end up shredding your wood as you carve. Carving this way is not nearly as efficient because the whole thing turns into more of a grating process than a smooth, gliding process.

You can purchase a strop at most carving supply stores or online. Listed on the next page are the different types of strops and their uses. You can also make your own strop fairly easily since it is basically a piece of leather on a stick (see the sidebar, "Make Your Own Strop," below).

Make Your Own Strop

You will need a piece of wood about 2" wide x ½" thick x 12" long. Cut a piece of leather—almost any type will work—to fit the lower portion of the wood, leaving the upper portion for a handle. I like to use tooling leather, which I get from my local shoe repair guy or saddle maker. It is smooth on one side, rough on the other side, and approximately ³⁄₁₆" thick. A thicker piece of leather adds to the durability of the strop. Glue the leather onto the strop with some contact cement, and you're good to go.

A lot of times you will see leather on both sides of a strop. One side will have the rough side of the leather out, and the other side will have the smooth side out. In stropping, you move from the rough side, which takes off more material, over to the smoother side, which refines the whole process.

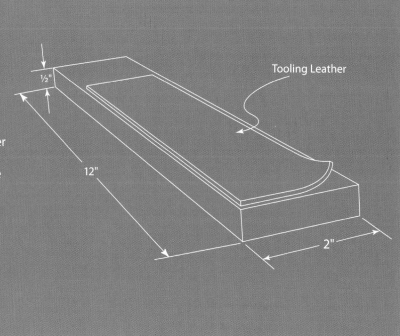

Tooling Leather

½"

12"

2"

types of strops

There are a variety of strops available from simple strops that have general uses to specialty strops that are designed to help you hone specific tools. Following is a brief overview of some of the most common types.

Many people use honing compound in conjunction with their strops. Honing compound helps enhance and speed up the polishing process. This compound, an abrasive powder that comes in a variety of forms, can be used with any of these strops.

Basic strop: A strop is a length of leather fastened to a wooden handle. Many strops are two sided: The rough side of the leather faces out on one side; the smooth side faces out on the other side. This type of strop is perfect for knives. Because gouges and V-tools have curved or angled interior surfaces, they require a different type of strop.

Butz strop: This specialized strop has flat surfaces for stropping knives as well as a curved edge for stropping the inside surfaces of gouges and an angled edge for stropping the inside surfaces of V-tools. While the Butz strop is a good choice, it is more expensive than the basic strop. The "green stuff" on this strop is honing compound.

Slip strop: This two-sided strop is made of wood and includes a number of curved and angled profiles to facilitate polishing the inside surfaces of a variety of gouges. This strop requires honing compound. Simply apply a honing compound to the shaped wooden surfaces and strop the tools over those surfaces. A slip strop also has two smaller leather strips for stropping. This strop is versatile and economically priced.

Basic strop. This simple strop is perfect for stropping knives.

Butz strop. The curved and angled sides of this strop are used to sharpen gouges and V-tools. Use the flat surface to sharpen knives.

Slip strop. The two sides of this strop include a variety of surfaces for stropping gouges, V-tools, and knives.

safety equipment

Because carvers deal with razor-sharp tools, steps must be taken to protect both the tools and the carver. There are supplies that you can purchase or make that help you play it safe. Tool rolls and carving aprons are by no means new to the art of carving, but these items are very necessary and you should invest in them right up front.

A broad selection of commercially made items is available, ranging in price, styles, and materials. However, for the purpose of this book, I have specifically designed patterns for a tool roll and a carving apron with the beginner in mind. These exclusive designs are relatively easy and inexpensive to make, are highly effective at protecting the carver and the tools, and will serve you well for many years. For these projects, I combined the features that I found most useful and liked best. They are my personal favorites.

Other items you should consider purchasing are a Kevlar glove and thumb guards. We will discuss the importance of each of these safety items.

tool roll

You only have to drop your tool on a hard surface once—or slice a finger reaching for a tool—to realize the value of a tool roll. It is very disheartening to be all ready to jump right into a carving project only to pick up a chipped knife or worse, to cut yourself. Then, you are back to square one. If you go through all the trouble to sharpen and hone your tools, you do not want them dropping out of a bag onto the floor or banging against each other in a shoebox.

A well-designed tool roll is absolutely necessary for protecting your tools and you. I say "well-designed" because not all tool rolls are constructed with a flap that pulls down over the tops of the tools and keeps them from slipping out of the roll. I had difficulty finding one like that, so I settled for one without for a while.

The tool roll pattern I subsequently designed (see the sidebar, "How to Make a Tool Roll," page 20) includes that all-important extra flap to hold the tools in place, and I believe it makes all the difference. I also designed this roll so that even those with the most basic sewing skills should find it a snap to make.

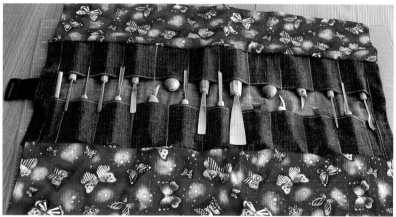

Tool roll. This well-designed tool roll snugly contains tools in an easy-to-transport bundle. By following the directions on page 20, you can easily make a tool roll to protect your tools (and you) from accidental damage.

carving apron

Some people say I am a bit of a samurai carver, which is probably true. I think a lot of women carvers tend to carve toward themselves because they do get better leverage that way. But I got tired of all the little holes in my shirts from where I got a little too close. That is where the carving apron comes in.

A carving apron is designed to protect your torso and lap from those little mishaps. Traditionally, these aprons have been all leather and cover you from your neck to your knees. Leather aprons provide the protection you need, but

Carving apron. This simple apron features a removable leather patch and provides lightweight, breathable, dye-free protection while carving.

tend to be very hot and cumbersome. Often the leather is dyed and the dye comes off on everything, including your carvings.

Personally, I have tried many different types of aprons until finally coming up with my own solution—a canvas apron with a removable leather patch just big enough to offer the right protection (see the sidebar, "How to Make a Carving Apron," page 26). I designed it so that the leather patch is attached to the apron with Velcro and can be removed. This means you can take off the leather patch for laundering or even replace it when you happen to carve through it too often. From a functionality standpoint, this apron is more comfortable and convenient, while at the same time offering you the protection you need. But whether you choose to buy one or make your own, you should not attempt to carve without a protective apron.

kevlar glove

The most significant thing you can do to carve safely is to carve with sharp tools. That's because sharp tools move more easily through wood using less force. However, they can be dangerous and mishaps do occur. I've had many nicks and scrapes on my hands but nothing serious because I take the proper precautions—like wearing a Kevlar reinforced carving glove.

Kevlar gloves are actually the gloves that meat cutters use. They are worn on the hand that does not hold the knife and are wonderfully cut resistant. You do need to note that the Kevlar glove is not puncture resistant. If you take your detail knife and stab your glove, it will go through. But in the course of carving if you just slip and the knife blade impacts the glove, it will deflect the blow and keep your hand and fingers safe.

You can find these gloves at a carving supply store or order directly online.

thumb guard

Although I don't use one, some people also wear a thumb guard on the hand that holds the knife for additional safety. Thumb guards come in many different variations but usually consist of a piece of leather attached to a piece of elastic that slips down over your thumb. You can also purchase reinforced self-sticking thumb and finger tape to wrap your fingers for further protection.

A thumb guard can be good for beginners just getting used to handling carving tools. If you use a thumb guard, be sure it fits snugly down over your thumb. If it does not fit tight, it is likely to slip and just be in the way.

health and focus

Never attempt carving while you are on medication that might affect your vision or coordination. And never carve when you are overtired because this will lead to mishaps. Woodcarving requires total focus and concentration, and anything that detracts from that is unadvisable. I think I maybe tend to overdo the safety thing, but I feel it is very important. And really, just using good common sense will help keep carving a safe, relaxing, and enjoyable pursuit.

Kevlar glove. A Kevlar reinforced carving glove will protect your hand from nicks and cuts during your carving sessions. However, remember that Kevlar gloves are not puncture resistant!

selecting wood

Wood to the carver is like clay to the potter, fabric to the quilter, or a canvas to the painter. It is the medium through which you express your art. For that reason, I suggest that you become familiar with the different types of woods available to woodcarvers and experiment with them until you find the woods that suit your specific needs and style.

Most woods fall into two categories: hard and soft. A simple way to learn the difference is to remember that hardwood comes from trees

Basswood. Perfect for beginners, this wood comes from linden trees and is sometimes called lime wood. Although classified as a hardwood, this pale, cream-colored wood is one of the softer hardwoods. It has a fine texture and a tight, even grain with very few knots or blemishes and holds details well.

Sugar pine. Classified as a softwood, sugar pine is another acceptable, easy-to-carve wood for beginners. However, your tools must be razor sharp or you run the risk of mushing up the details. For that reason, softer woods require tools with a longer bevel than those used on hardwoods. So unless you plan to have two separate sets of tools, it is best to focus on one wood type or the other, at least in the beginning.

Butternut. This wood is another interesting option for beginners. Although classified as a hardwood, it is considered to be of medium hardness with a medium-coarse texture and a beautiful grain pattern. Its coloration runs from cream to reddish brown.

with leaves that drop during the winter, such as maple, oak, walnut, and pecan. Softwood comes from trees that do not have leaves but rather needles, such as pine and fir trees. Then, within each category, there are many subcategories or degrees of hardness. For example, walnut and butternut are both hardwoods, but walnut is harder than butternut, making it more challenging to carve.

You might think that the softer the wood, the better it is for carving, but that is only true to an extent. Some softwoods like balsa are so soft that they often crush when you try to carve them and do not retain any detail. Pine is a softwood that's a little harder than balsa. Because of that, it might be an acceptable wood, but carving pine requires a different angle on your tools and the tools must be very sharp so that you don't mush up a face or detail. I recommend using basswood for your first project. The photos and information following will help you choose a wood for your subsequent projects.

wood grain

In choosing your wood, it is important to consider the grain of that particular piece of wood. Why? Because every time you carve across it, you run the risk of wood chipping off your carving, and that is certainly not what you want. So before you begin your carving project, pay attention to which way the grain is running. The wood grain always runs the length of the wood.

purchasing wood

You can purchase blocks of wood for carving that have already been processed and refined before you buy them. They are planed and cut into blocks of specific sizes and then air- or kiln-dried. These blocks of wood are available on the Internet or locally through carving supply stores and specialty wood stores that sell carving wood. If you are not sure what you need, spend some time browsing through catalogs or go online to see what is available. The Internet is a valuable resource both in learning what is available to beginning carvers and also for ordering wood online.

Most of my experience has been in buying carving wood, so your experience may be slightly different if you are buying wood through a construction lumber dealer. For me, basswood purchased from a lumberyard has not been great to carve. I recommend buying wood from a source that specializes in carving wood.

Wood is usually sold by the board foot. Whether you purchase your wood online, through a catalog store, or even at a lumberyard, make sure you get what you want by always using this wood measurement equation:

Thickness x Width x Length

The first measurement given in ordering wood is the thickness of the wood in inches (two-inch stock refers to wood that is two inches thick). The second measurement given is the width of the wood in inches. The final measurement is the length of the wood in inches.

One board foot is 1 inch thick x 12 inches wide x 12 inches long. To determine board feet, multiply length (in inches) by width (in inches). Multiply that number by the thickness of the board (in inches), then divide by 144, which is the number of square inches in one board foot.

Example:

6 (length) x 14 (width) = 84

84 x 2 (thickness) = 168

168 ÷ 144 (number of square inches in one board foot) = 1.167 board feet

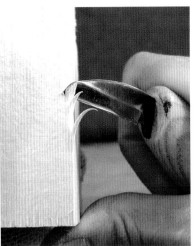

Carving with the grain. To determine the grain of the wood, test carve on the edge of a block. When you are carving with the grain, the knife or gouge will move easily through the wood and produce little wood curls and smooth facets. The tool will naturally rise back up to the surface of the wood. Carving against the grain will feel as if your tool is being pulled deeper into the wood. Experiment with a couple of pieces of wood, and you will be able to determine the grain of the wood easily. Remember that the grain may change within any particular block.

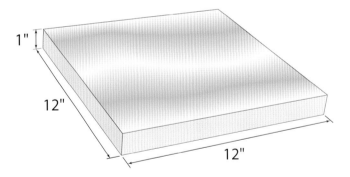

Board feet. One board foot equals 1 inch thick x 12 inches wide x 12 inches long

found wood

Of course, you may want to gather your carving materials straight from Mother Nature herself. It's fun and soothing to the soul to get out there and scavenge around in the great outdoors looking for the perfect piece of wood. With any luck you might locate some diamond willow branches or a sturdy piece of cottonwood bark or a curiously shaped cypress knee. All of these would make wonderful carvings. But they do require extra preparation on your part to remove (or peel) bark, clean them, and dry them.

Found woods can be very enjoyable to carve, but keep in mind that they all contain sand and grit that remain even after their initial cleaning.

This will require a bit more maintenance on your part because your tools will dull more quickly. Still, the emotional rewards of carving that special piece of wood you found yourself may be worth the extra effort. If you like the look of found wood but don't want to find it yourself, you can find this type of wood on the Internet also.

cutouts and boxes

With the growing popularity of what the craft stores are calling "wood décor," it is now even easier to find premade boxes and precut shapes. With a little investigating, many of these products are now available in basswood. Premade boxes come in all sorts of shapes and sizes—from plain old rectangles to attractive hearts and octagons. Precut shapes, often called "cutouts," come in just about any shape you can imagine.

If you have a scroll saw, you can cut these shapes on your own. If not, you can purchase them to use in your carving or you might seek out a woodcarving or scroll sawing group for someone who is willing to saw up whatever shapes you need. The *Bunny Box* (see page 100) in Part IV of this book uses a premade basswood box purchased from a local craft store. The *Aztec Angels* (see page 96) and the *Welcome Sign* (see page 130) make use of cutouts. Be sure to ask what type of wood the boxes and the cutouts are made from. You'll want to use only those that are made from real wood, not plywood or pressed wood.

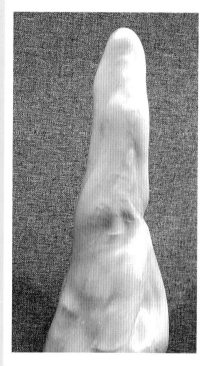
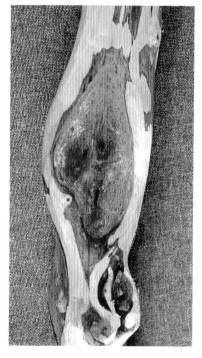

Found wood. Found wood like this cypress knee, diamond willow branch, and section of cottonwood bark are relatively easy to locate and fun to carve, despite the extra effort required to prepare them for carving.

painting and finishing supplies

I may not know exactly how I want to finish a piece until I am actually done carving it. Because of this, I like to have a variety of finishing supplies at hand. That way, when a project is carved, I'll have everything I need to finish it.

In this section, we'll go over some different finishing supplies just to show you some of the options. Following is a basic list of the items I use to finish my carvings. Of course, if you decide that you only like a few types of finishes, you don't need to have all of these items on hand.

Acrylic paints: Acrylic paints come in a wide variety of colors and are readily available in carving supply and craft supply stores. They are quick drying and are easily blended with other colors or thinned with water. I like the two-ounce bottles of acrylic paint and pretty much exclusively use Delta Ceramcoat paints. A 6" x 6" piece of folded wax paper serves as my palette.

Water-based satin varnish: This product is great for woods with appealing grain patterns, or it can be used over a painted carving. Varnish can be found at all paint, hardware, and craft stores. Be sure to look for a satin finish; you don't want your finished piece to be too glossy. The water-based type makes for easy cleanup.

Wood stain: Stains come in a variety of finishes—oak, maple, walnut, cherry, and pine, for example—and are perfect for accentuating woods with visible grain patterns. These can be found wherever hardware and paint supplies are sold.

Danish oil: This product stains, seals and protects in a one-step process. The finish penetrates and hardens in the wood as opposed to sitting on top of it and creates the look of a hand-rubbed finish. Always wear rubber gloves when working with this product because it contains resins that should not be absorbed into the skin.

Finishing supplies. Having a variety of painting and finishing supplies on hand gives you options when you are ready to finish a carving.

Boiled linseed oil: An oil finish is ideal for showing off the wood grain. This product is easy to use and creates a wonderful result. Be sure to read the safety precautions on the product package when using it.

Paste wax: Paste wax gives a hard, durable finish to carvings with a natural finish. Paste wax can be used as a final finish to any previously applied painting or finishing technique.

Antiquing medium and retarder: There are many extender and retarder products on the market. I like to use Jo Sonja's antiquing medium and retarder and mix it with equal parts of any acrylic paint to create an antiquing mixture. The mixture is painted on and quickly wiped off with a soft dry cloth until the desired effect is achieved.

Disposable foam brushes: These inexpensive brushes are great for finishes, like stain, that would ruin your good paintbrushes.

Paintbrushes: For acrylic paint, I recommend shader brushes in sizes 2, 6, and 8, such as Loew-Cornell Series #4300, and a liner brush in size 1, such as Loew-Cornell Series #4050. For varnishing, I use a ¾" wash brush from the Loew-Cornell Series #4550. Any old, worn-out brush or a cloth will work well for applying oil. It is important to use a good quality paintbrush because a wonderful carving can be ruined when poorly painted.

other supplies

Clean cloths: Rags are used for applying finishes. Old, worn-out T-shirts can be great for applying antiquing and oil finishes. White T-shirts are best; I have had some problems with colored fuzz when using a colored T-shirt.

Rubber gloves: I only wear rubber gloves when I do oil finishes or work with stain. Oil finishes are messy, and Danish oil products contain resins that you do not want absorbed into your body. I prefer latex gloves to the heavy rubber ones you would wear to wash dishes. Latex gloves are thin and allow you to maintain your dexterity while wearing them.

Cheesecloth: Used in conjunction with paste wax, cheesecloth is a great tool for getting an even coat of paste wax on a carving.

Carving is my business as well as my passion. That's why I want to make it as efficient and as streamlined as possible. When I start a piece, I like to be sure that I have everything I need at the outset so that I can complete it without running around looking for additional items I may need to get the job done.

In the safety section, I listed some things that would help ensure a comfortable and safe carving experience. These next items are additional supplies that you may want to keep on hand to assist with your carving projects. Many of them are common items you may already have around the house. I suggest you collect them and keep them in one central location so you know where they are when you need them.

12" flexible ruler: Measuring takes the guesswork out of proportions and lengths. My favorite measuring instrument is a clear two-inch-wide sewing ruler. Because it is clear, you can see exactly what you are measuring underneath.

Pencil: I use a pencil in every carving project to draw the reference and pattern lines on each block of wood. A common No. 2 pencil works well for this task.

Graphite paper: Graphite paper is used to transfer a pattern to the block of wood. This can be found in stationary or craft supply stores.

Tissue paper: Keep a supply of tissue paper on hand if you choose to trace the patterns from the book directly onto tissue paper. You may find it easier to photocopy the patterns.

Quick grip all-purpose adhesive: I much prefer this type of glue to typical wood glue. Quick grip glue, like the type from Beacon Adhesives, typically dries clear and bonds in about 15 minutes.

Wood repair epoxy putty: Everybody makes an occasional mistake. This putty is very handy for those places where I might not have carved as well as I had hoped. It fills in unwanted gouges, low spots, or gaps in blocks. It allows one more opportunity to salvage a project that might otherwise be in jeopardy.

Carpenter's wood filler: Slightly different in consistency from epoxy putty, this too proves handy for fixing up carving boo-boos, such as a stray V-tooled trench, or for blending the seam between two laminated pieces of wood.

Fine-grit sandpaper: This is great for removing what I call stray wood "hairies," which are tiny, ragged wood fibers that loosen up during the carving process.

Stylus: A stylus is very versatile and can be used to trace patterns and to apply tiny dots of paint, glue, and other liquids. If you use this tool to trace around patterns when transferring them to a block of wood, it keeps the patterns nice so they can be reused. Styluses come in a variety of point widths, making them handy for many uses. They are often found in craft stores.

Square: A drafting square comes in handy when assembling the candlestick on page 92 to ensure that it is straight vertically.

Cyanoacrylate adhesive: Otherwise known as Super Glue, this too can facilitate all kinds of repairs.

Wood glue: If you don't have quick grip glue, traditional wood glue will suffice. I will also use wood glue when laminating several large boards together. For the most part, I find the quick grip glue much more efficient than wood glue and use it almost exclusively.

Old toothbrush: There is nothing quite like a soft old toothbrush for brushing away wood hairies and tiny wood chips from carvings. I keep several of them around because they do such a great job.

Additional supplies. Many common household items can be very useful in your carving pursuits.

Quilter's template plastic grid: I carried over this tool from my quilting projects because it worked so much better than using paper patterns. On occasion, you may want to use a template to make more than one of the same carving. For example, you may want to carve a *Bunny Box* (see page 100) for several different people for Christmas or to sell at craft fairs. If you transfer the pattern onto the gridded plastic, rather than paper or card stock, it lasts forever, and you can make as many of the exact same thing as you wish. Cut into a one-inch-wide-by-six-inch-long strip, gridded template plastic can be a flexible ruler. It will wrap around carvings that would otherwise be difficult to measure. I keep several of these around and have given them to all of my carving friends.

Power drill and ¼" drill bit: I use a drill to make small holes in wood so that I can insert dowels into them. This allows me to fit two or more blocks together like I did to make the candlestick on page 92.

Manual drill: I also use a manual drill that holds small diameter bits, such as ¹⁄₁₆" drill bits. I use the manual drill for wire doweling and attaching small parts.

how to make a tool roll

Follow these basic sewing instructions (or pass the information on to a friend who can sew) to create your own tool roll. This roll will hold up to 19 standard-size carving tools with lengths up to 11" and widths up to 35 mm (1½"). It also nicely accommodates intermediate and palm tools.

Note: These instructions assume a basic knowledge of sewing techniques.

supplies

finished size

Rolled: 12" x 4½"

Unrolled: 25" x 32"

fabric:

l yd. denim or canvas fabric, at least 45" wide

1 yd. lightweight cotton print fabric, at least 45" wide

notions:

Coordinating sewing thread

Coordinating topstitching thread

1 2" two-bar strap fastener (I used a Looploc fastener, found at outdoor recreation stores)

½ yd. 2"-wide sew-on Velcro

Scissors

Straight pins

Sewing machine with zigzag capabilities

White chalk pencil

Rotary cutter and mat (optional)

1 Cut the following pieces from denim or canvas: 1 panel, 13" x 36", for the backer panel and 2 panels, 8" x 30", for the tool pocket panels. Cut the following from the cotton print fabric: 4 panels, 8" x 32", for the flaps.

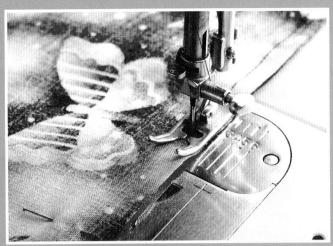

2 With right sides together, pin together two panels of cotton print fabric. Stitch three sides using a ¼" seam allowance. Leave one 32" side open. Using the same process, stitch the remaining cotton print panels together. These will become the flaps that afford extra cushioning and protection for the tools.

3 Turn the panels right side out and press them flat with an iron.

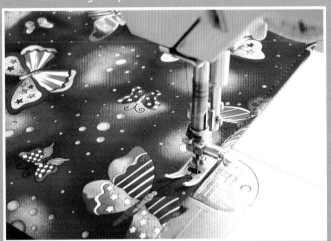

4 Topstitch ¼" from the edge on the three stitched sides of both panels.

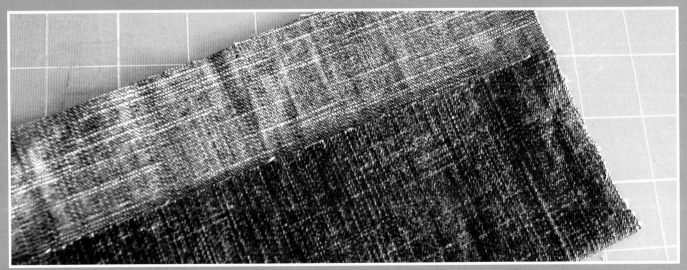

5 Fold the 8" x 30" denim or canvas panel lengthwise, wrong sides together, so that one side is 3½" and the other side is 4½". The 4½" side will be the right side of the folded piece. Press with an iron. This folded piece will become a tool pocket.

6 Place the folded piece with the 4½" side (the right side) up. Topstitch ¼" from the folded edge of the right side to create the pocket panel. Repeat Steps 5 and 6 with the other denim panel.

7 Using a chalk pencil, mark 3" increments, as shown, on the right side of one pocket panel. On the other panel, mark the first section at 1½"; then, mark the remainder of the sections at 3" increments.

8 When the pocket panels are placed folded edge to folded edge, the tool pockets are staggered.

9 Fold and press ½" on each short end of the 13" x 36" backer panel, as shown.

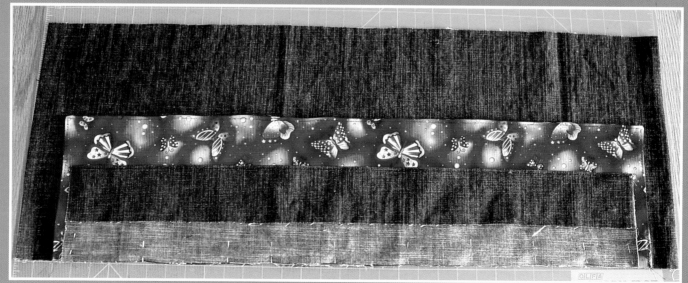

10 Layer the fabric pieces as follows: Place the 13" x 36" denim backer panel right side up on the table. Measure in 2" from the left side of the backer panel. Place a flap piece on top of the backer panel, matching the raw edges at the bottom.

Measure in ½" from the left side of the flap piece. Top with the pocket panel face down, matching raw edges to the other panels. Pin the panels in place along the raw edges at the bottom.

11 Repeat this stacking sequence with the other flap and tool pocket panel, as shown. Pin the panels in place.

12 Stitch both long edges with a ½" seam allowance, as shown. Be sure to stitch all the way from one edge of the backer panel to the other.

13 Pull the flap panels out and turn the entire piece over. Fold the pocket panels back in so the wrong side of the pocket panel faces the wrong side of the backer panel.

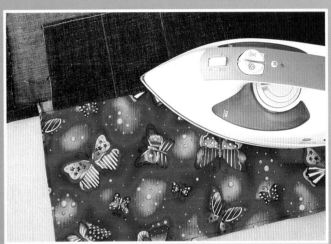

14 Press the seams with an iron.

15 Topstitch close to the bottom seam of the pocket panel.

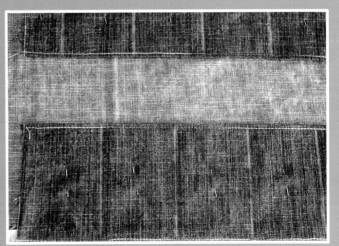

16 Place pins between the pocket stitch lines to hold the pieces in place.

17 Beginning at the bottom of the pocket panel, sew along each line previously marked with chalk to create individual tool pockets. Remember to backstitch at the beginning and end of each stitch line.

18 Fold the denim ends over the pocket panels, as shown. Pin in place.

19 Topstitch close to the edge, as shown.

20 The pockets and the edges of the tool roll should look like this.

21 Fold the flaps over the tool pocket panels and topstitch close to the edges, as shown.

22 Thread a 15" length of loop Velcro through the Looploc, as shown. Pin in place.

23 Stitch the Looploc in place using a wide zigzag stitch. Stitch and backstitch this seam several times to reinforce it.

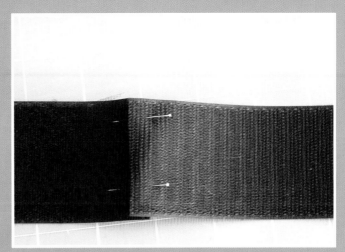

24 Pin a 6" length of hook Velcro to the opposite end of the loop Velcro that you attached to the Looploc, right side up on each.

25 Stitch in place using a wide zigzag stitch. Stitch and backstitch this seam several times to reinforce it.

26 Round the remaining free end of the Velcro with scissors, as shown.

27 Pin the Velcro band, right side up, to the outside of tool roll, as shown, leaving the Looploc end and 2½" of the band extending past the edge of the tool roll. Stitch the band in place, stitching and backstitching the seam several times to reinforce it.

28 Place the tools in the roll, as shown in the opening photos. Cover the tools with the flaps. This protects the tools and keeps them from sliding out of the tool roll. Roll and cinch it closed with the Velcro band, as shown in the opening photo.

how to make a carving apron

Follow these basic sewing instructions (or pass the information on to a friend who can sew) to make your own carving apron. **Note:** These instructions assume a basic knowledge of sewing techniques.

supplies

fabric:

1 yd. denim or canvas fabric, at least 45" wide

8" x 7½" leather patch

notions:

Coordinating sewing thread

Coordinating topstitching thread

2 1" side-release buckles (find at outdoor recreation stores like REI)

2¾ yds. soft link 1" polyproplene webbing

½ yd. 2"-wide sew-on Velcro

Scissors

Straight pins

Sewing machine with zigzag capability

Rotary cutter and mat (optional)

Candle and matches

White chalk pencil

1 Cut the following pieces:
Cut 2 pieces from denim using apron pattern on page 31 .
Cut 2 36" lengths of 1" webbing.
Cut 2 5" lengths of 1" webbing.

2 Transfer the outlines of the leather patch and the straps to the front of one of the apron panels using a white chalk pencil.

3 To keep the webbing from fraying, pass the cut ends of the webbing through the flame of a candle. This will slightly melt and fuse the ends.

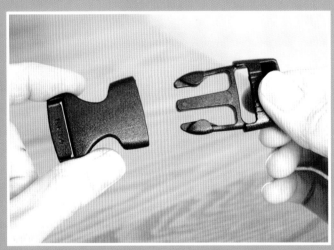

4 Separate the side-release buckle.

5 Thread the female ends through the 5" pieces of webbing.

6 Match the cut edges of the webbing and pin them to each side of the apron, as indicated on the pattern. Using a wide zigzag stitch, machine baste the webbing to the apron front.

7 Using a wide zigzag stitch, machine baste the 36" straps to the apron top, as indicated on the pattern.

8 Pin the long straps to the middle of the apron to keep them out of the way during the remaining apron construction.

9 Pin the apron sections together, right sides facing. Stitch around the apron using a ½" seam allowance. Leave an 8" opening on the lower edge of apron for turning the apron right side out. Stitch slowly over the apron straps.

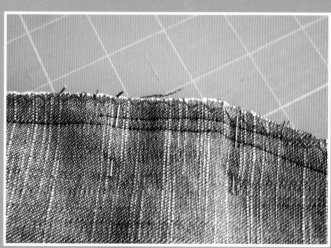

10 Sew a second row of stitching ¼" from the apron edge at all points where the straps are attached.

11 Trim the excess off the corners.

12 Turn the apron over and press all of the seams flat.

13 Pin the 7½" sections of loop Velcro on the apron front, as indicated on the pattern. Sew the Velcro on using a zigzag stitch. Sew around each section of Velcro twice to reinforce it.

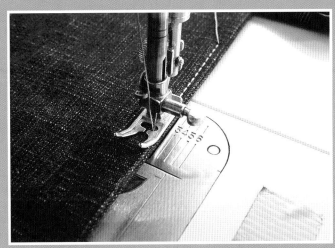

14 Topstitch the apron as desired.

15 Thread the male end of the buckle through the strap webbing, as shown.

16 Reconnect the male and female ends of the buckles. This completes the sewing of the apron.

17 I have the two sections of hook Velcro sewn to the 8" x 7½" piece of tooling leather at my local shoe repair shop.

18 The leather is attached to the apron with Velcro.

The finished carving apron is comfortable, convenient, and helps protect you and your clothes from any little mishaps.

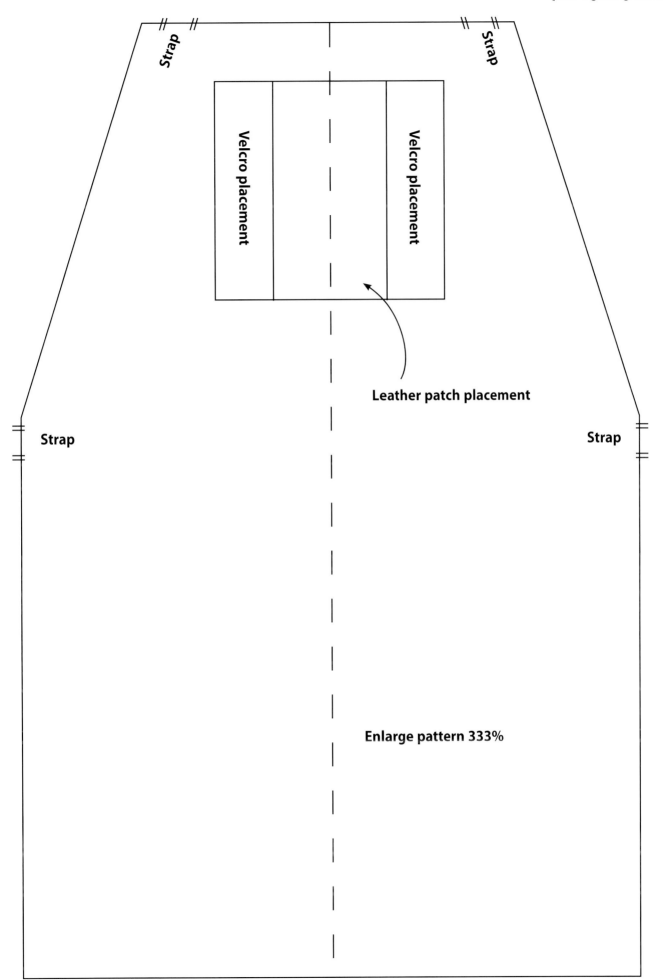

Strap

Strap

Velcro placement

Velcro placement

Leather patch placement

Strap

Strap

Enlarge pattern 333%

basic
techniques

For the purposes of this book, we are not going to band saw out the preliminary shapes, as many carvers do. Rather, we will go straight to the block of wood. If you purchase a block of wood intended for carving purposes, there is very little, if any, preparation involved. Precut blocks come dried and ready for pattern transfer. Many wood sellers will gladly cut wood to whatever dimension you request.

I'll show you the basics of using patterns, several common cuts, and painting and finishing techniques. Combine these skills with the information you learned in Part I, "Getting Started," on page 1, and you're one step closer to being ready to carve your first project.

transferring patterns

For beginners, being able to choose and use the right pattern is important for a successful carving experience. Many carving books include patterns for projects. There are also pattern packets available. These packets usually include a pattern for a band sawn shape and photos of the four different sides of the project. And that's it!

In my experience, pattern packets are of little use to a person with minimal carving experience since there are no directions for how to get from the band sawn shape to the finished product. That is why I included step-by-step photos in this book. They take you through the entire process, not merely provide you with the pattern. I start with easy patterns so that, if you follow these directions, your finished project should look reasonably like mine. A pattern is a great starting place, and I encourage you to use my patterns as a foundation. Then, eventually, when you are ready, use your own creativity to develop a style of your own.

There are many different pattern transfer methods, and you will learn five of them in the subsequent pages. The degree of accuracy needed dictates whether tracing is adequate or if a more precise method needs to be employed. If you want cutouts that are virtually identical, then a template is required. If you want a sign with a nice, square, even border, using the pattern as a guide works best. Below are the five methods covered in this text.

adding registration lines

Though this technique is not used by itself, adding registration lines is very useful in conjunction with other methods of pattern transfer. It allows you to find the center point on the top and the bottom of a block of wood. Since a frequent challenge with beginning carvers is the ability to keep the carving centered, adding registration marks and then referring back to them during the carving process aids in keeping the carving centered on the block of wood. To use this method, simply connect opposite corners on the top and the bottom of each block of wood to create an X. The middle of that X marks the center point of the wood. This method can be used on all projects carved from blocks of wood.

Registration lines. An X drawn from corner to corner on the top and the bottom of the block will help you find the center of the wood.

Photocopy or tissue paper transfer. Sandwich a piece of graphite paper between a photocopy or a tissue paper copy of the pattern and the wood to transfer patterns.

tissue paper transfer

The easiest way to use most of the patterns in this book is to photocopy them. However, if you do not have access to a photocopy machine, you can trace the patterns onto tissue paper by placing a piece of tissue paper over the pattern and tracing the pattern. Then, simply sandwich a piece of graphite paper, carbon side down, between the pattern and the wood and trace over the lines with a stylus. This method can be used on all projects carved from blocks of wood.

Tag board templates. A tag board template is more durable than a paper pattern. Trace the pattern onto tag board by sandwiching a piece of graphite paper between the pattern and the tag board. Trace around the tag board template to transfer the pattern to the wood.

Gridded plastic templates. Trace the pattern onto a piece of gridded plastic, and then cut it out for a long-lasting, flexible template.

templates

Templates are used to create wooden cutouts. An example of this is the rabbit on the *Bunny Box* project in this book, found on page 100. The advantage of the template is that you can use it multiple times and get the exact same outline or shape on the wood each time. If you wanted to sell a bunch of the *Bunny Box* projects at a craft fair, you would use this method for consistency in your work. If you were to use a tissue paper transfer, you might get different but similar shapes each time.

patterns as guides

Any time you want to transfer a pattern that consists basically of straight lines, you can use the pattern to mark each line at the corner point of the wood and then connect the dots with a ruler. This method makes for a more precise pattern transfer. I use this technique on the *Welcome Sign* on page 130. The border of squares will be much more precise if you look at the pattern, use it to measure the depth of the border, transfer that measurement to the wood, and then use a ruler to make a nice, even, precise border line. Use the pattern again to make tiny slash marks for each square and again connect the slash marks using a ruler to end up with a crisp, accurate border instead of tracing the pattern and ending up with wiggly, squiggly lines. Using the pattern as a guide is more accurate, but it takes more time to transfer a pattern this way.

freehand transfer

Some patterns can't be transferred with a ruler or graphite paper. The *Cypress Knee Santa* project on page 118 is a perfect example. Every cypress knee is different, so, while the idea of the pattern will work, the actual lines might not. In those cases, you'll need to transfer your pattern freehand. Take a good look at the finished example and use your best judgment to transfer the lines to your piece of wood. Odds are that if you're using freehand transfer, the pattern doesn't have to be exact. After all, I have yet to meet a Santa Claus with the same proportions as the *Cypress Knee Santa*!

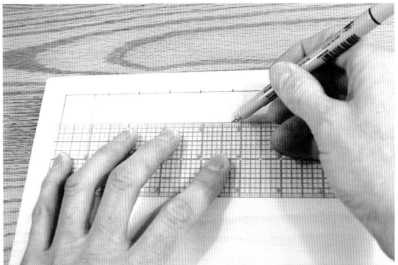

Using the pattern. Mark guidelines on the wood using the pattern as a guide and connect these points with a ruler. Any remaining details can be transferred directly to the wood by sandwiching a piece of graphite paper between the paper and the wood.

making the basic cuts

Now we're ready to make our first cuts! You'll only have to deal with a few basic cuts to carve the projects featured in this book. We'll go over each of them individually here. Plan to refer back to this section as you work your way through the step-by-step instructions for each project.

Before you practice these cuts, you'll need to determine the grain of the wood to ensure that you carve *with* the grain rather than *against* it (see "Wood Grain" on page 14). Carving against the grain is difficult and will not produce good results. You also need to examine your wood for any chips, splits, or knots and try to avoid those areas or incorporate them into the portions to be carved away.

the stop cut

Carving is really a pretty basic thing—scoring a line and then carving back to that line. The scored line is called your *stop cut*. A stop cut is a very simple but extremely useful technique.

Shade the area. I draw a series of closely spaced parallel lines on the wood to shade the area where wood will be removed. I will refer throughout the book to these shaded areas. You may choose whether or not you wish to actually add the shading lines or just refer to the photos that show them. Here, I have shaded an area to be removed that is ¾" deep x 2" wide x ¾" long.

Make a stop cut. Pull the bench knife along the line you traced onto your wood. This is called "scoring the wood," and it creates a stop cut. Score the line to about ¹⁄₁₆". Start at one edge and continue across the wood until you are about ¼" away from the other edge. Score back from the other edge to meet the line you just scored.

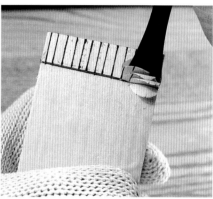

Carve back to the stop cut. With a #3 ⅝" or a #3 ⅞" gouge, carve back to the line you scored, removing thin slices of wood. This is called "carving back to the stop cut." The stop cut we made will naturally interrupt the forward motion of the gouge. Note that the slices of wood may not come off at this point. We'll take care of that in the next step. Never pull the slices off.

Deepen the stop cut. Retrace the original stop cut with a bench knife or use the gouge to deepen the stop cut and release these thin slices of wood.

Repeat the process. Continue removing thin slices of wood and deepening the stop cut.

The finished cut. When all of the wood in the shaded area has been removed, you should have a flat and level ledge.

the push cut

Sometimes you'll be carving off the end of the block. You'll want to use a controlled cut, not the kind of cut you'd make when peeling a carrot with a vegetable peeler! To control your cut, place the knife in your hand and cut only as far as your thumb will reach without moving the rest of your hand.

the pull cut

The pull cut is the opposite of the push cut. To make this cut, you will be pulling the knife toward you in almost the same motion as you would use to pare an apple. The one major difference is the placement of the thumb of your carving hand. Always—and I do mean always—keep it out of the path of your knife. Carving knives are very sharp. Don't rely on a thumb guard to protect you from a cut.

cutting with a gouge

Gouges cut in two different ways: by hand and by mallet.

To make a cut with a gouge by hand, hold the gouge firmly in the palm of your hand and wrap your fingers around the handle. Bring the gouge toward you, with the palm of your hand facing up, as you cut. Again, keep the fingers and wrist of your other hand and your body out of the path of the gouge and use a small range of motion. This is a controlled cut.

To make a cut with a gouge using a mallet, place the gouge against the wood and tap the mallet to move the gouge through the wood. This cut should only be done when the wood can be held securely to the workbench. *Never* use this technique when you are holding the wood in your lap.

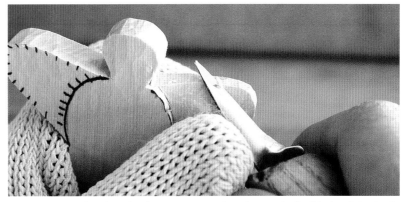

Push cut. Use the thumb of your opposite hand to push the blade of the knife away from you.

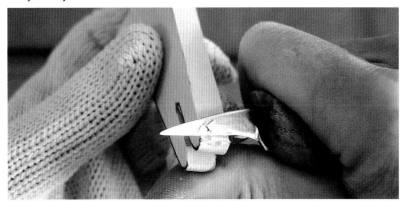

Pull cut. Pull the knife toward you, being careful to keep the thumb of your carving hand and your opposite hand out of the path of the knife.

Gouge cut. Bring the gouge toward you, keeping your opposite hand out of the path of the gouge.

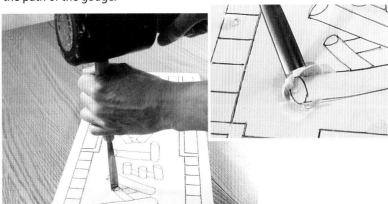

Gouge cut with a mallet. Once the wood is held securely to the workbench, place the gouge against the wood and tap on the gouge's handle with the mallet.

how to strop a knife

Now that you've made some first cuts with your tools, it's time to strop them. Stropping is easy to do and is definitely well worth the time you put into it. As I mentioned earlier, stropping is simply the process of honing the blade on a polishing surface to repolish the edges of the tool. A tool with highly polished edges will move through wood smoothly. You will learn to recognize that, when your tool feels like it is beginning to drag through the wood, it is time to strop.

Stroping the blade 50 times on one side and 50 times on the other side will take only a few minutes, but it makes all the difference. Some carvers suggest that you strop your tools five minutes for every 30 minutes of carving. My carving is always much more enjoyable if I just take that five-minute preparation to get my tools back up to speed.

Remember, you can choose to strop with or without honing compound. If you do use honing compound, the type you choose—solid bars, cream, or others—is entirely up to you. Any type will help speed up the process.

What's a bevel?

The bevel of a knife simply refers to the angles on the sharpened edge. When you strop, be sure that the bevel, not the side, of the knife is placed firmly against the leather.

The edge created by the two bevels makes a knife sharp. Keeping the bevels highly polished will ensure your knife is razor sharp.

1. Hold the strop in your left hand. Place the blade of the knife on the strop near the handle with the beveled edge of the knife toward you.

2. Push the knife along the leather to the far end of the strop with firm pressure. Make sure the bevel of the knife is in contact with the leather as you push. When you reach the end, lift the knife and return it to the leather near the handle. Repeat this step 50 times.

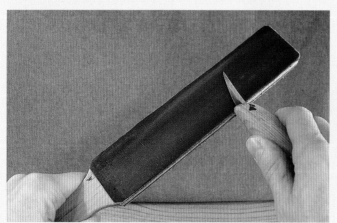

3. Now hold the knife at the far end of the strop with the beveled edge of the knife away from you.

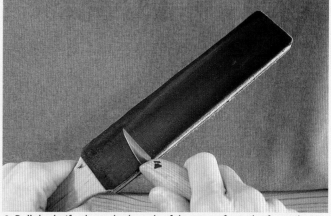

4. Pull the knife along the length of the strop, from the far end toward the handle, using firm pressure. Make sure the bevel is in contact with the leather as you pull. When you reach the handle, lift the knife and return it to the far end of the strop. Repeat this step 50 times.

how to strop a gouge

Stropping a gouge is similar to stropping a knife, but all edges of the curved surface of the gouge must be polished. You can choose to strop with or without honing compound. I've used it for this demonstration. My honing compound is a micro-fine green chromium oxide compound. It comes in a bar, and I rub it over the strop before I begin the stropping process. If you choose a slip strop, use the honing compound that comes with the strop when you hone your tools.

If you use a slip strop and all surfaces of the bevel contact the channel of the strop, you do not need to rotate the gouge or strop the gouge in sections. The inside surface of the gouge must also be stropped. The slip strop has a variety of shaped profiles to fit the inside surfaces of a variety of gouges.

Curved bevel

A gouge has one less bevel than a knife, but it can be more challenging to strop because you must hone all sections of the curved bevel. As with stropping a knife, the bevel of a gouge, not its sides, need to be in contact with the leather.

The gouge has only one beveled edge, but the curve of that bevel can make it more challenging to strop.

Using a Flat Strop

1. If you are using a flat strop, you need to strop the gouge in sections. Hold the gouge at the far end of the strop with the left bevel of the gouge on the strop. Pull the gouge toward you, making sure the left side of the bevel is in contact with the leather. Repeat 50 times.

2. Rotate the gouge slightly so that the center part of the bevel is in contact with the strop leather. Strop 50 times, pulling the gouge toward you.

3. Finally, rotate the gouge so that the right edge of the bevel is in contact with the strop leather. Strop 50 times, pulling the gouge toward you. The larger-sweep gouges will require more rotations to address all sections of the gouge.

Using a Slip Strop

1. Fit the gouge, rounded side down, into the far edge of the appropriate channel. Pull the gouge down the length of the strop with firm pressure. When you reach the end of the strop, lift the gouge and return it to the far end of the strop. Repeat 50 times.

2. Find the surface that is most like the inside surface of the gouge you wish to strop. Place the gouge at the far side of the strop, inside surface on the curved strop surface. Pull the gouge down the length of the strop with firm pressure. When you reach the end, lift the gouge and return it to the far end of the strop. Repeat 50 times.

painting and finishing techniques

After you have completed your carving project, you must decide how you want to finish it. Among your finishing choices are painting, staining, antiquing, or applying oil and paste wax. You may choose any one of these or a combination to suit your purposes. In choosing, you should consider your personal taste, the type of carving, what it will be used for, the kind of wood, if it will be handled frequently, and whether it will be exposed to the elements.

Finishing products produce beautiful results but must be used with care. Before we talk about specific finishes, be sure to read the sidebar below.

Safety Tips

■ Remember to always follow the manufacturer's safety precautions when applying any of these finishes.

■ Wear latex gloves because finishes are messy and may contain resins and other elements that could be harmful if absorbed into your body.

■ Work in a well-ventilated area. Many of these finishes are combustible and have harmful vapors.

■ If you use cloth rags to apply oil, always lay them out flat and allow them to dry before disposing of them. Oil products produce heat as they dry and, if not properly used, can spontaneously combust. Wadding up an oily cloth and throwing it in a trash can is creating the potential for a fire.

painting

Any wood can be painted with acrylic, oil, or latex paint. As I mentioned earlier, basswood is one of the most popular woods for carving, but it does not have the beautiful wood grain of other woods. Because the wood is so plain, items carved out of basswood are typically painted.

Personally, I find acrylic paint to be the most convenient because it cleans up very easily. Your color choices may be subtle or bold, dramatic or fun, whatever emotion you wish to express. Avoid using full-strength paint directly out of the bottle because it is too thick, does not flow, and fills in fine details that you probably don't want filled in. Instead, thin the paint with water to make it easier to work with. Remember to use good-quality brushes for your carvings.

If you decide to paint your carving, it then needs to be finished with varnish or paste wax. If the carving will be exposed to the elements (outside), finish with a spar varnish.

To paint your carvings:

Step 1: Apply a wash that is one part water and one part acrylic paint. Using a wash for the first coat allows you to easily get paint into all of the cracks and crevices and allows the paint to soak into the wood a little bit. Allow the first coat to dry 15 minutes before applying the second coat.

Step 2: Follow up with a second coat of paint that is thinned with water only slightly to the consistency of cream. The water allows the paint to flow more easily, but the mixture still provides adequate color coverage.

A painted finish. Paint adds color and provides a small amount of protection for your carving. Basswood projects are often painted because of their mild grain patterns. A painted project is typically finished with varnish or paste wax.

staining

There may be occasions when you would like your carving to take on the appearance of another wood. To achieve that effect, you would use a wood stain. Normally, stains are applied to woods that have a visible grain pattern, but they may be used on any wood. Stains are thinner in consistency than paint and are often applied with a cloth or a disposable foam brush in the same manner as paint. Since stain can be messy and will stay on your brush, avoid using good paintbrushes for staining. Stains come in a variety of finishes—oak, maple, walnut, cherry, and pine, for example.

To stain your carvings:

Step 1: Apply the stain per the manufacturer's directions. Use a disposable foam brush to apply the first coat of stain. Typically, the wood is covered with an even, thin coat of stain. Maintain an even color as you are applying the stain.

Step 2: A second coat may be required depending on the richness of color you desire. Allow each coat to dry thoroughly before adding the next. A stained project will typically be finished with varnish or paste wax.

A stained finish.
Plain basswood can take on the appearance of any wood when finished with wood stain.

varnishing

There are many types of varnish. For the projects in this book, a water-based varnish is a good choice because it is easy to apply. Varnishing is another method of finishing that does not block out the wood grain, but it works best over paint. It basically involves applying thin coats of varnish with a paintbrush. Typically, the more thin coats you apply, the nicer the finish. If you just put on one thick coat, you may get a lot of air bubbles, so multiple thin coats work best.

Clean up with water-based varnish is very easy and requires only soap and water. Carvings finished with water-based varnish would be for interior use only. If your carving will be exposed to the elements, you need to finish it with a spar varnish product. Apply the product according to the manufacturer's directions.

To varnish a carving:

Step 1: Using a ¾" wash brush, apply one thin coat of varnish (one part water-based varnish and one part water) to the project after the paint is dry. Varnish may foam as you apply it.

Step 2: After a minute or two, brush over the varnished area to smooth out any bubbles. Wait 15 minutes.

Step 3: Then, apply a second thin coat. Again brush away any remaining bubbles after a minute or two. Allow the piece to dry overnight.

A varnished finish.
Water-based varnish may foam as it is applied. Varnish protects painted surfaces and adds a rich luster to projects.

antiquing

If you like the look that age brings to a carving, you may want to consider antiquing. It is easy to do and nicely highlights the details of your carving. The antiquing process is done over a painted and varnished piece. Quite different and not necessarily desirable results will be experienced if the painted piece is not varnished before the antiquing is applied. Once you have painted and varnished a piece, you can make an antiquing mixture out of any color of paint that will complement your carving by adding that color paint to antiquing medium/retarder. Typically, you would use a brown shade of paint. My favorite is a mixture of one part spice brown, one part burnt sienna, and two parts antiquing medium/retarder. For more subtle antiquing, use one part dark flesh and one part antiquing medium. Since antiquing involves wiping off the bulk of the antiquing mixture, try not to leave it on any longer than you have to. On larger pieces, I will antique one section at a time. The antiquing mixture allows you several minutes of working time, but I don't like to risk having it dry before I am able to remove as much of the mixture as I want. I used this technique on the *Welcome Sign* carving project found on page 130 in this book.

To antique your carving:

Step 1: Create an antiquing mixture to suit your project.

Step 2: After the antiquing mixture is ready, use a worn-out brush to completely cover the carving (or sections of a large carving) with the antiquing mixture. Use an old brush, and don't be timid about mashing it into the cracks and crevices and using it to really scrub the antiquing mixture on the carving. Completely covering the carving with antiquing mixture is the key to the antiquing process. Here, I am using an antiquing mixture of one part spice brown, one part burnt sienna, and two parts antiquing medium/retarder.

Step 3: With a soft cloth (or a cotton swab in small areas), wipe off the antiquing mixture until the piece has the look you want. Allow the piece to dry thoroughly.

An antiqued finish.
Antiquing is easy to do, and it emphasizes the details of your carving.

oil

Oil finishes have been used for centuries to preserve wood and to bring out its natural beauty. Unlike finishes that remain on the surface, oil penetrates the wood and is absorbed into the fibers where it hardens and forms a strong finish. Oil finishes are easy to apply and offer added protection to the wood. Linseed oil and tung oil cure and work well as finishes. If you use linseed oil, be sure to use boiled linseed oil because it has an added drying agent that helps the finish dry faster. Without this additive, the finish could take a week or more to dry. Boiled linseed oil often takes a week or less. Tung oil does not require a drying agent and cures in several days.

To create an oil finish for your piece:

Step 1: Apply oil to the carving with an old paintbrush or a soft cloth. Allow the carving to soak up the oil for about an hour.

Step 2: Then, using a soft cloth, wipe off any remaining oil. Allow the carving to dry for 12 hours.

Step 3: Apply a second coat of oil. After 15 minutes, wipe off any remaining oil. Allow the oil to cure for several days. Once the oil has cured, the carving can be left as it is or you can apply a coat of paste wax to finish it.

An oil finish. Oil finishes bring out the wood grain and offer a strong finish to protect your carving.

Combining Finishes

Different combinations of finishes can achieve different effects. Since, for example, acrylic paint dries very flat, some further finish is needed. Here are the most common ways, and the best orders, to use finishes on a project.

Finishing Possibilities for Painted Projects	Finishing Possibilities for Unpainted Projects
Paint, then varnish	Oil
Paint, then varnish, then antique	Oil, then paste wax
Paint, then varnish, then antique, then paste wax	Stain (oil based), then oil, then paste wax

paste wax

To add a rich luster to your carving, enhance its beauty, and give it a nice, hard finish, you might want to apply a paste wax. Paste waxes were very popular when everyone had wood floors, but now you do not hear about them much. Minwax makes a very nice paste wax that works well on woodcarvings. I used it on the *Shell Paperweight* project found on page 124 in this book. Paste wax can be used as a final finish on any carving. For example, you can use it alone, over stain, or over a painted surface.

To add a paste wax finish:

Step 1: Place some paste wax in a double layer of cheesecloth and rub it over the carving. Use this method to apply a thin, even coat of paste wax to the entire carving. Allow the wax to dry 10 to 15 minutes.

Step 2: Then, polish the carving with a soft, clean cloth. Use some elbow grease to get a highly polished shine.

A wax finish. This finish adds luster and helps protect your carving. Paste wax is also a very versatile finish that can be used in conjunction with many other finishing techniques.

doweling

Some carvings consist of auxiliary pieces of wood that are adhered to the main piece of wood. Doweling is a way to ensure that these connections will be strong.

For this book, we'll use two different doweling techniques. One uses a wooden dowel to connect two parts of a carving; the other uses a wire to connect the pieces. Both methods use glue to make sure the connection stays tight.

Doweling is done most often after a carving has been painted and finished. It is much easier to paint and finish the pieces separately and then attach them than it is to apply paint or finish to a fully assembled piece. The exception to this would be when arms or other integral parts of the carving are added. It is necessary to add them and blend them into the main carving before you paint or finish.

wood doweling

Wood doweling uses lengths of ¼" dowel rods to connect the pieces of the carving. The process is simple, but you have to do some preliminary planning to get it right. Take the time to dry fit the pieces together and trace the outlines as explained at the right. Otherwise you may end up with holes on the outside of your carving instead of at the joint where they belong. This technique can be used to join the practice blocks into a candlestick in Part III, Skill-Building Exercises, on page 93.

wire doweling

When attaching small pieces, wire can be substituted for wooden dowel. Again, be sure to dry fit all of the pieces before you glue. I'll give you an example of how this works by showing you how to connect a nose to a snowman's face.

Wood Doweling

Trace. Dry fit the pieces you wish to join together. Transfer the outline of the top piece to the bottom piece.

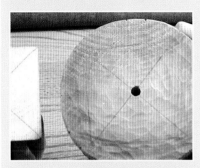

Drill. Draw lines to connect opposite corners or edges to find the center point of each piece. Draw these lines on the bottom of the top piece and on the top of the bottom piece. Plan carefully! With a hand drill and ¼" drill bit, drill a ½"-deep hole at the center point of each piece.

Glue. Glue a 1" length of ¼" dowel in the top piece using wood glue. Add glue to the bottom piece under where the top piece will sit. Fit the pieces together. Allow them to dry.

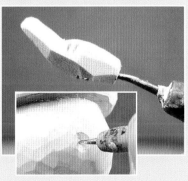

Wire Doweling

Drill holes. Using a stylus or a manual hand drill and a ¹⁄₁₆" drill bit, make a hole in the center of what will be the snowman's carrot nose. Then, make a corresponding hole in the snowman's face.

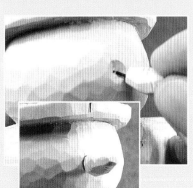

Glue. With cyanoacrylate glue, adhere a ½" length of baling wire into the hole in the carrot. Dry fit the carrot with the wire into the corresponding hole in Snowman's face. Add more cyanoacrylate glue to the remaining end of the wire, and then insert the carrot into the snowman's face, as shown.

skill-building
exercises

The key to successful carving is developing, practicing, and building your carving skills. In this chapter, you'll learn the basic shapes and decorative techniques that serve as the foundation for all carving projects by using eight blocks of wood, each different in pattern and in graduating degrees of difficulty. Each skill builds on the one preceding it, so you'll want to complete the projects in order. In the process, you will learn what you need to know to tackle more advanced projects. You'll also learn how to use various carving tools, such as gouges, bench knives, and detail knives.

When the blocks are all completed, you can use them in a variety of practical or decorative ways. Be patient, stay focused, and have fun.

block 1 round shapes

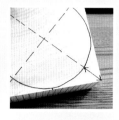

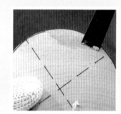

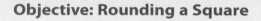

Objective: Rounding a Square

In this first block project, you will remove small layers of wood to first create

a round shape and then create a cylinder with smooth, even sides. Learning

this basic technique will prove valuable to you in the future because it is

used frequently for all kinds of carving projects. It also introduces you to

the gouge in a way that helps you to feel comfortable and at ease using it.

So relax, take your time, and follow the steps below.

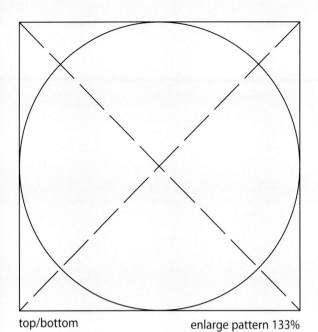

top/bottom   enlarge pattern 133%

© Cyndi Joslyn

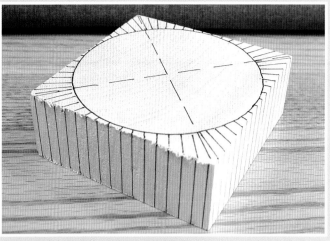

1 Transfer the pattern and the registration lines to the top and bottom of the block, and add shading if you wish to show the wood that needs to be removed.

2 Notice how much more wood must be removed from the corners of the block than the sides to create "round."

tools and supplies

4" x 4" x 1½" basswood block

Graphite paper

Stylus

Ruler

#3 ⅞" or #3 ⅝" gouge

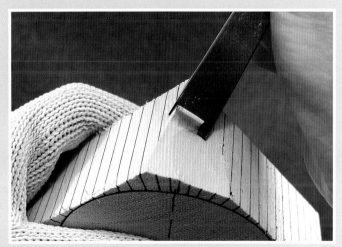

3 Using the #3 ⅞" gouge, remove the wood to the edge of the circle.

4 Turn the block over and remove the wood to the edge of the other circle.

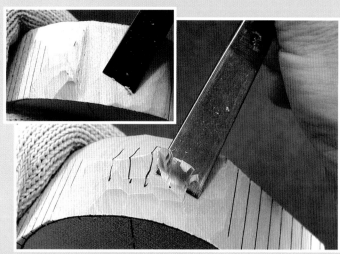

5 Blend the remaining wood together to create a cylinder.

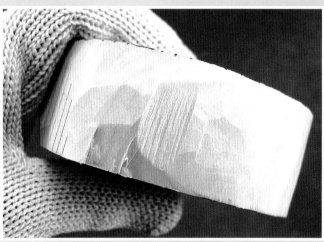

6 If you notice the wood coming off in stringy sections as you are carving, you are carving against the grain of the wood.

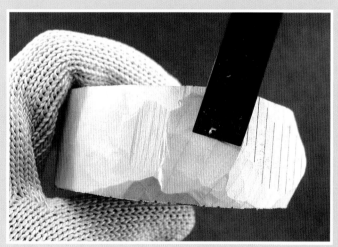

7 Turn the piece over and carve in the other direction, and you will notice the wood carves in a much smoother fashion. Your goal is to create a uniformly round cylinder with sides that are perpendicular to the base.

8 Roll the cylinder on a table or other hard surface to see how uniform the sides are. Notice how the block comes into contact with the table. This will show you if there are high areas that need further attention.

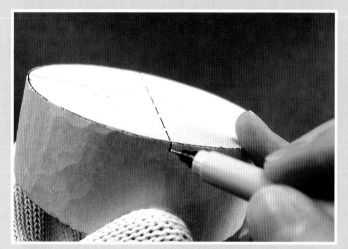

9 Mark the registration lines on the sides of the cylinder.

10 Using the #3 ⅞" gouge, shave away the saw marks on the top of the block.

11 Using the registration marks on the sides of the cylinder, reestablish the center point on the top of the block.

12 This block will be revisited later to add an incised design on the sides of the cylinder.

Applying What You've Learned

Once you've learned to make a cylinder, you are ready to use it as a building block. This tube-like shape is a basic component that can be used in all kinds of carving projects. This Santa, for example, has several cylinders in its construction. The body, top hat, and lower arms are all cylinders.

block 2 angled sides

Objective: Creating Angled Sides

In this exercise, you will learn how to remove wood to create a block with angled

sides. Carving flat, even angles is another skill you need to master in order to

tackle more advanced projects. We will use the same #3 ⅞" gouge as in the first

project so you can become more comfortable with that particular tool.

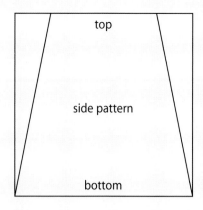

top

side pattern

bottom

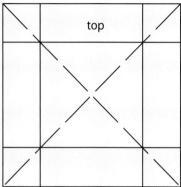

top

enlarge pattern 133%

© Cyndi Joslyn

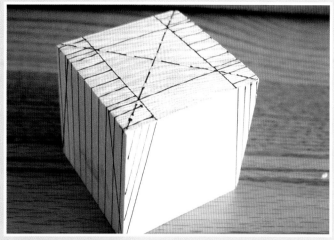

1 Transfer the pattern and the registration lines to the top and bottom of the block. Add shading to show where wood will be removed.

2 Using a #3 ⅞" gouge, begin removing the wood along the edge of the shaded area.

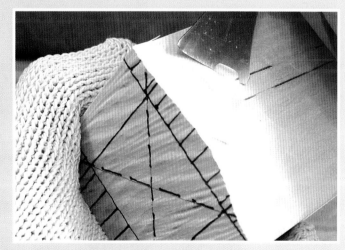

3 Continue to remove the wood across the face of the block.

tools and supplies

2½" x 2½" x 2½" basswood block

Graphite paper

Stylus

Ruler

#3 ⅞" or #3 ⅝" gouge

4 Use the pattern lines on all three sides of the block as guides to achieve a flat, angled side.

5 Pull a ruler over the carved surface to check for high spots.

6 Continue to use a #3 ⅞" gouge to remove the wood from the opposite side of the block.

7 All sides should be evenly angled and flat.

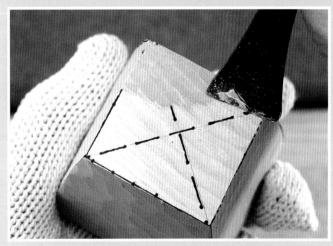

8 Use the #3 ⅞" gouge to shave the top of the block to remove any saw marks.

9 Redraw the lines connecting the opposite corners to reestablish the center point on the top and bottom of the block. This block will be revisited later to add a relief-carved design to the sides of the block.

Applying What You've Learned

Now that you know how to create a block with angled sides, you can tackle more advanced projects. This birdhouse, for example, uses the flat, even angles of a trapezoid in its design. It is similar to Block 2, only upside down.

block 3 ball

Objective: Creating a Ball

Now that you are a bit more familiar with the basic carving process, let's tackle

something a little more complicated that requires a variety of tools. For this

project, you will create a round ball from a cylinder using the gouge and a bench

knife. You will also learn an easy step-by-step technique for carving a simple

decorative border on the ball using a detail knife and a #7 4 mm gouge.

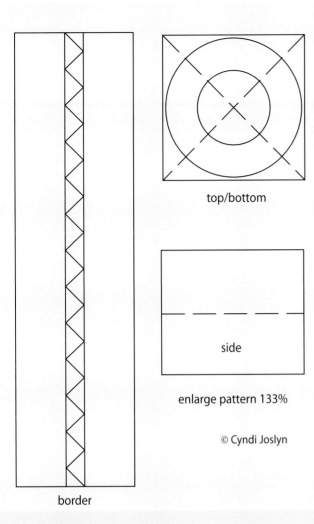

top/bottom

side

enlarge pattern 133%

© Cyndi Joslyn

border

tools and supplies

2" x 2" x 1¾" basswood block

Graphite paper

Stylus

Ruler

#3 ⅞" or #3 ⅝" gouge

Bench knife

Detail knife

#7 4 mm (³⁄₁₆") gouge

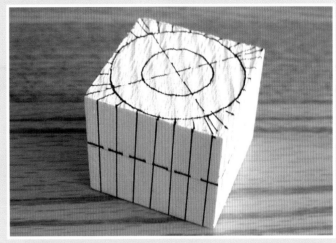

1 Transfer the pattern and the registration lines to the top and bottom of the block. Draw a centerline on the sides of the block. Add the shading to show where the wood is to be removed.

2 Using the #3 ⅞" gouge, start to remove the wood from the corners. Remember how much more wood must be removed from the corners of the block than from the sides to create a round shape.

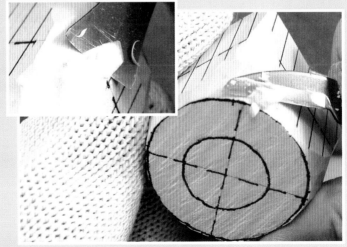

3 Alternate between the gouge and the bench knife to carve the cylinder. This carving process is identical to the process you learned as you carved the first practice block.

4 The cylinder should be evenly rounded with perpendicular sides, as shown. Roll the cylinder along the table to test its roundness.

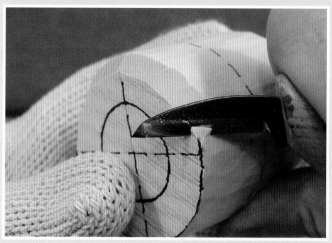

5 Redraw the centerline on the sides of the cylinder. With the bench knife, begin rounding the ends of the cylinder.

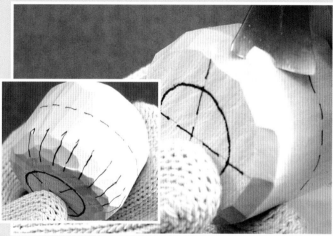

6 Use the #3 ⅞" gouge to continue rounding the block. Remove the wood from the shaded area (see inset), alternating between the gouge and the bench knife. Note that, even after removing a couple of layers of wood in the shaded area, the ball is still basically square.

7 Continue to remove layers until the ball is truly round. Round the ball right up to the edges of the circles on the ends of the block.

8 The ball should be evenly rounded in all directions except for the flat areas within the end circles. Notice how the centerline you added in Step 5 is still visible.

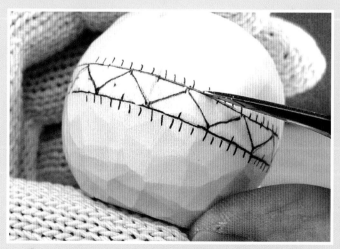

9 Use the centerline to position the band pattern. Carve away the centerline before adding the triangular design to the band. With a detail knife, score all of the lines.

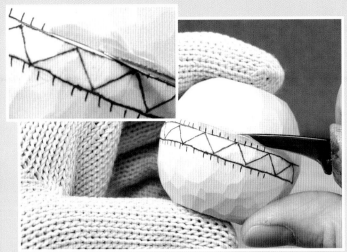

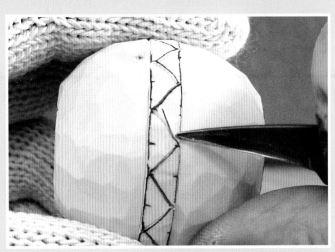

10 Use the stop cutting technique to score the outside lines as shown, and carve a thin layer of wood outside the line that marks the band. Then, rescore the original line to release this thin layer of wood.

11 With the detail knife, carve very thin slices of wood away from each side of all of the diagonal lines, as shown.

12 Round the sharp edges of the design band with the detail knife.

13 Using a #7 4 mm gouge, make a shallow scoop in the center of each triangle, as shown. If you don't have a #7 4 mm gouge, you can leave off the scoop inside the triangle.

14 Your finished ball should look like this. Notice that I did not sand the ball to remove all of the knife and gouge marks. Because I like the way the carved facets look on my carvings, I rarely sand my carvings.

Applying What You've Learned

The ball, which is carved from a cylinder, is another of the basic shapes that can be incorporated in almost any project. Evenly rounded balls are everywhere. You'll find them here in the cat's paws.

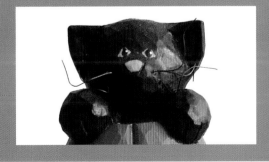

block 4 low relief carving

Objective: Carving in Low Relief

By carving this block, you will learn how to create low relief carvings. Low relief

is a carving that is done in definable layers so that the entire carved surface has

a shallow look to it. During this process, we will use the #7 4 mm gouge and a

simple technique that adds additional depth and texture to your carvings.

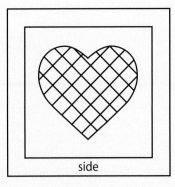

side

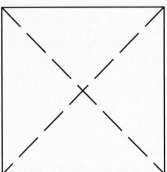

top/bottom

© Cyndi Joslyn

tools and supplies

1¾" x 1¾" x 1¾" basswood block

Graphite paper

Stylus

Ruler

#3 ⅞" or #3 ⅝" gouge

Detail knife

#7 4 mm gouge

1 mm V-tool

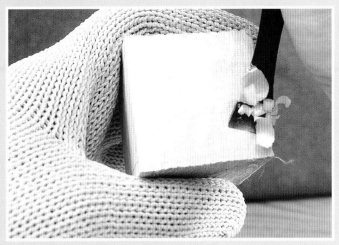

1 Using #3 ⅝" gouge, shave wood off the faces on all sides of the block. This is especially handy on areas that may not end up being carved: It will allow all sides of the wood to have subtle carved facets.

2 Transfer the pattern and registration lines to the top, bottom, and sides of the block.

3 Score around all pattern lines (the heart and the square border) with the detail knife. Begin to remove the wood from the shaded area.

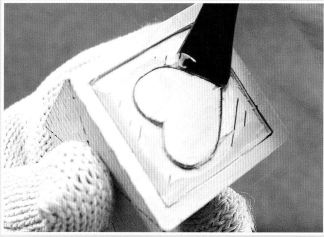

4 Continue to remove the wood from the shaded area with the detail knife and the #3 ⅝" gouge to a depth of approximately 1⁄16".

5 Use #7 4 mm gouge to texture the background behind the heart, as shown. If you don't have a #7 4 mm gouge, leave the block as is. The texture will just not be as defined.

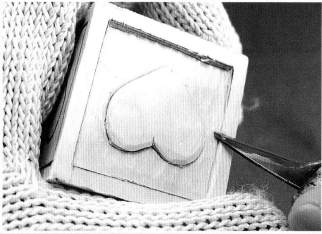

6 Round the edge of the heart and the edge of the border with the detail knife.

7 Using a 1 mm V-tool, carve lines of crosshatching on the heart, as shown. Carve slowly and try to carve each line in one stroke. Keep all of the V-tooled lines equal in depth. Lift up the V-tool ever so slightly as you near the edge of the heart so that you don't extend the crosshatching into the background.

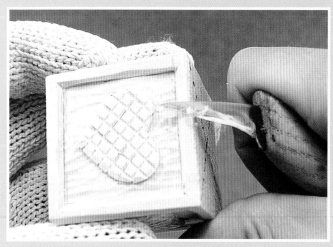

8 Round the sharp edges of the border and the corners of the block with the detail knife.

9 The block is finished. With a pencil, redraw the lines connecting the opposite corners to reestablish the center point on the top and the bottom of the block.

Applying What You've Learned

Low relief carving is a simple technique that adds additional depth and texture to your carvings. Use it to make carved blocks in any number of shapes, sizes, and designs. ABC blocks or blocks with a holiday theme, like these, are popular applications of this technique.

block 5 pillar

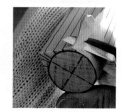

Objective: Maintaining an Even Circumference

Using tools you should now be comfortable with, we move on to a more difficult project—that of creating a long, decorative pillar. You must first begin by removing wood from your block to create the actual pillar. The challenge lies in maintaining the circumference as well as the perpendicular sides throughout the entire length of the pillar. The length of this project will give you experience with wood grain, which can and does change within the same block of wood.

Another skill presented in this project is carving a design on the pillar. The technique shown here is simple, yet it offers a very gratifying, dramatic effect.

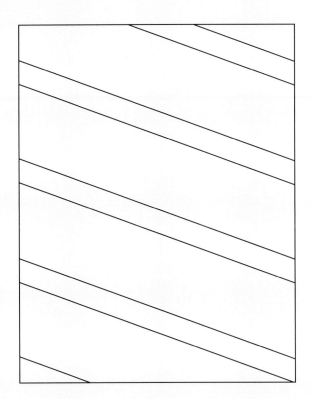

enlarge pattern 133%

© Cyndi Joslyn

top/bottom

tools and supplies

1¼" x 1¼" x 5" basswood block

Graphite paper

Stylus

Ruler or flexible ruler

Bench knife

#3 ⅞" or #3 ⅝" gouge

Detail knife

1 Transfer the pattern and the registration lines to the top and bottom of the block. Add the shaded areas to show where wood will be removed.

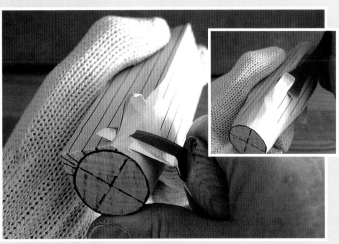

2 Using a bench knife, begin removing wood in the shaded area outside the circle. Continue to remove wood with the #3 ⅞" gouge.

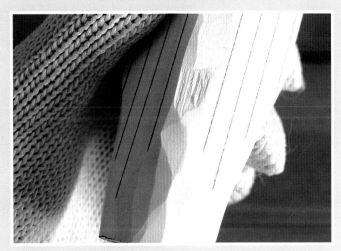

3 Watch for changes in wood grain from one area to another. If the wood looks stringy or ragged as you are carving, you may be carving against the grain. Turn the wood upside down and carve in the other direction. Carving with the grain produces smooth facets.

4 The goal in carving the pillar is to maintain the roundness throughout the length of the piece and also to maintain the circumference of the wood.

5 The carved pillar should have a circumference of 3⅞". Measure it with a flexible ruler or a piece of string that you can then measure with a straight ruler. The ruler made from gridded plastic, discussed in Part One on page 19, works great for this kind of measurement.

6 Transfer the pattern to the wood, matching the spirals at the edges of the pattern.

7 Score all of the spiral lines with either a bench knife or a detail knife. Remove the wood in the shaded areas on both sides of the spiral bands using the stop cutting technique.

8 For safety reasons, don't score off the end of the pillar. Stop about 1" from the edge, turn the block over, and score back from the edge.

9 With a detail knife, round the edges of the spiral bands, as shown. Remember to stop and carve back as you near the edge of the pillar.

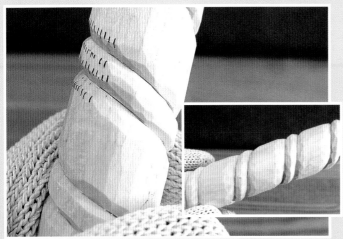

10 Further round the pillar using the detail knife, as shown. Your progress to this point should match the pillar shown in the inset.

11 Mark a pattern of 1" segments followed by two ¼" segments around the spiral band. Score these lines with the detail knife.

12 With a detail knife, remove thin wedges of wood on each side of the scored lines on the spiral band.

13 Round and shape the band segments, as shown. The finished block maintains the roundedness of the cylinder with the added decoration of the spiral band.

Applying What You've Learned

Take a basic long cylinder and carve a design on it to create a decorative pillar. The technique is simple and gratifying. This Santa's walking stick, carved to give a very dramatic effect, is an example of a decorative pillar.

block 6 chip carving

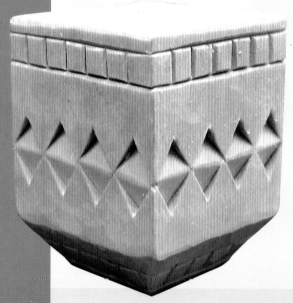

Objective: Creating Patterns

In this exercise, you will practice carving angled faces, similar to those on Block 2, page 54. The difference here is that an incised border will decorate the top and bottom of the block. I will also introduce you to the art of chip carving.

Chip carving is a very old form of carving that creates elaborate patterns with various arrangements of carved angles. For example, the basic chip-carved triangle consists of two vertical stop cuts and one horizontal slicing cut. The deepest part of the triangle is at its point (apex), graduating to a shallow cut at the baseline of the triangle. Then, a horizontal slicing cut removes the chip.

For this project, you will use a special tool called a skew knife, or a stab knife. These techniques are a little more difficult, so take your time and pay close attention.

© Cyndi Joslyn

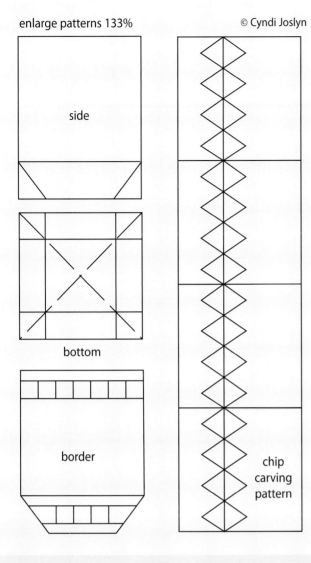

side

bottom

border

chip
carving
pattern

tools and supplies

1¾" x 1¾" x 2¼" basswood block

Photocopy of chip carving pattern

Graphite paper

Stylus

Ruler

#3 ⅝" gouge

#3 ⅞" gouge

Detail knife

Skew knife (sometimes called a stab knife)

Rubber cement

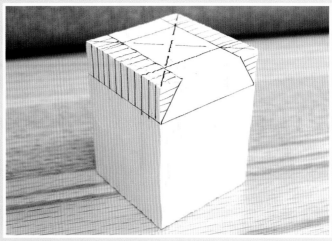

1 Using #3 ⅝" gouge, shave off the faces of all sides of the block. All sides of the wood, even if they are not carved, will then have subtle, carved facets. Transfer the pattern to the block, draw the registration lines, and add the shading to show where the wood will be removed.

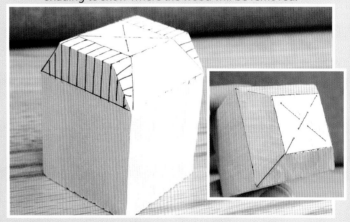

2 Using the #3 ⅝" gouge, remove the wood in the shaded area (see Block 2, page 54). Then, mark the angles on the remaining two sides of the block. Remove the wood in the shaded areas. The bottom of the block should have evenly angled sides when you are finished with this step.

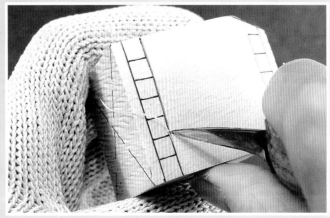

3 Transfer the border patterns to the sides of the block. Score all of the lines in the top and bottom border designs with the bench or the detail knife. With a detail knife, remove a very thin slice of wood on each side of each line using the stop cutting technique.

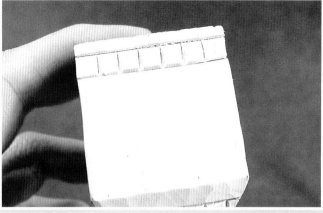

4 Compare your work on the incised border pattern to this model. Plan ahead and make sure that the lines on each side meet at the corners. Use care when carving toward the corners to ensure that the lines will meet.

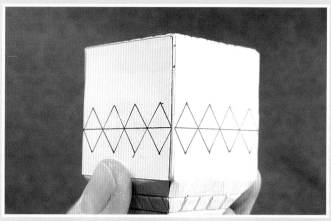

5 Photocopy the chip carving pattern, page 71, to use for the chip carved portion of the block. Cut the pattern into sections for each side, and glue the pattern sections to the block with rubber cement. Rubber cement works well because it holds the pattern in place, but allows for easy removal when the carving is complete.

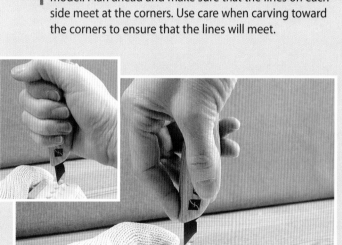

6 These photographs show two ways to safely hold a skew knife. Experiment to see which way feels best to you.

7 Stab the point of the skew knife into the apex of the triangle. Insert the knife point approximately ⅛" into the wood.

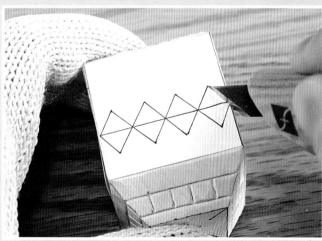

8 With the motion you would use to operate a paper cutter, rock your hand down toward the centerline following the line on the pattern. You have just created a stop cut. Pull the knife out.

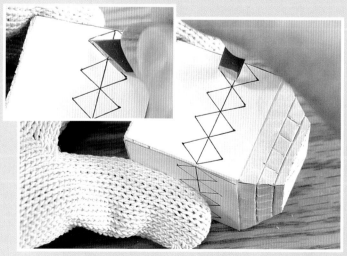

9 Begin again at the apex of the triangle and repeat the stab-and-rock motion for the left side of the triangle. You have just created a second stop cut.

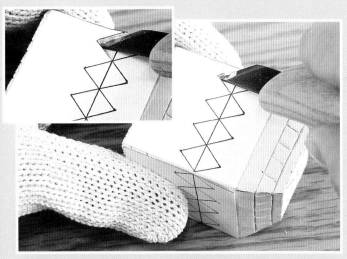

10 Using the skew knife or a detail knife held at a 10- to 15-degree angle, remove the chip you created with the stop cuts. Try to use one slicing cut to remove the chip. As a beginner, however, you may wish to do a series of horizontal cuts to avoid making the horizontal cut too deep.

11 It may be helpful to do all the stop cuts in a row before you do the horizontal slicing cuts. Then, when you do the slicing cut, you can maintain the angle of the knife from triangle to triangle.

12 Carve all of the triangles on one row; then, turn the block upside down and carve the remaining triangles. The goal is to have the same depth at the apex points of all of the triangles.

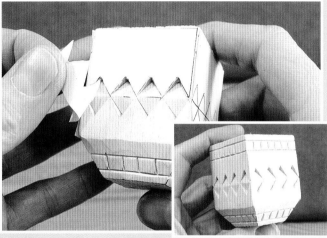

13 When you are finished carving, remove the pattern and clean off any rubber cement residue that remains on the block. Compare your progress to this point with this model.

14 Using a #3 ⅞" gouge, shave off the saw marks on top of the block to complete the project. The finished block has evenly incised square borders and a tidy middle border of chip-carved triangles.

Applying What You've Learned

Once you have learned how to carve angled chips, you can progress to more advanced chip carving projects. Chip carving can be used to decorate any number of items. This tissue box holder from Dennis Moor's *Chip Carver's Workbook* is just one example of what you can do.

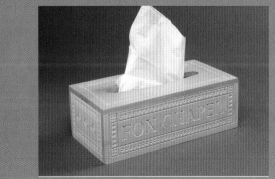

block 7 segments

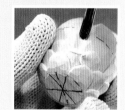

Objective: Dividing a Ball into Segments

For this project, you will incorporate the same skill you learned in Block 3 (on page 58), which was carving a ball from a cylinder using a gouge and a bench knife. In addition, I demonstrate another technique for creating a decorative scale design as well as how to divide the ball into rounded vertical sections.

This project is more complex, but the results will showcase your progress.

Remember, each new skill mastered adds to your carving repertoire.

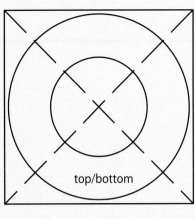

top/bottom

scale pattern

© Cyndi Joslyn

tools and supplies

2" x 2" x 2" basswood block

Graphite paper

Stylus and pencil

Ruler

Plastic grid template

Scissors

#3 ⅞" or #3 ⅝"gouge

Detail knife

Bench knife

#12 4 mm V-tool (optional; use the bench
   knife if you don't have the V-tool)

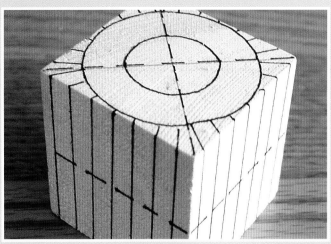

1 Transfer the pattern to the top and bottom of the block. Draw in the horizontal centerline on all sides of the block. Add the shaded areas that show where the wood will be removed.

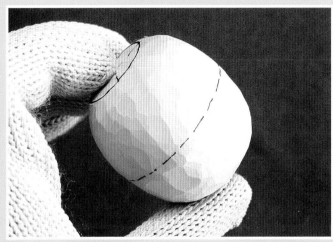

2 This ball starts with the same steps as the ball in Block 3 on page 58. Follow the instructions for Block 3 through Step 8 of that demonstration. The ball should be evenly rounded in all directions, except for the flat areas within the end circles.

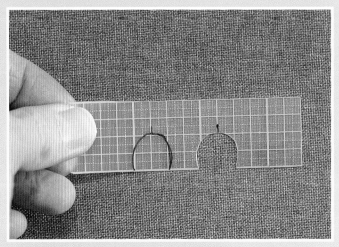

3 Trace the pattern for the scale design onto the plastic grid template. With scissors, cut out the pattern.

4 Divide the end circles into six equal sections. Trace the scale design on each of the six sections, as shown.

5 Measure up ⅝" from the end circle between the two scales on the first row and trace six more scales. Measure up ⅜" from the high point of the first row of scales and trace six more scales, as shown.

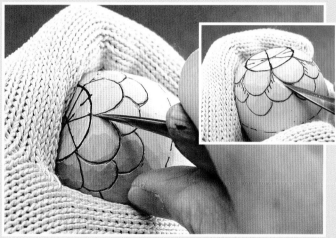

6 Score around each scale with a detail knife. On the first row, remove wood from the shaded area between the scales with the detail knife, as shown.

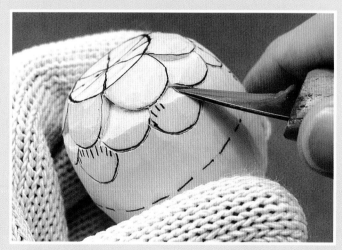

7 Continue to remove wood from the shaded area at the top of the scales on row three, as shown. Note that I am holding the block upside down as I carve it. The wood you are removing in this step is above the row of scales in row one, which is the bottom of the scales in row three.

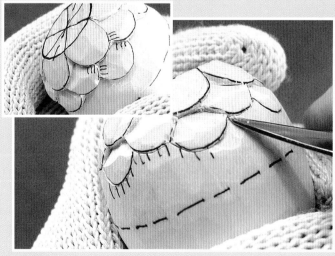

8 Remove the wood from the shaded areas. The goal is to have definition around each scale.

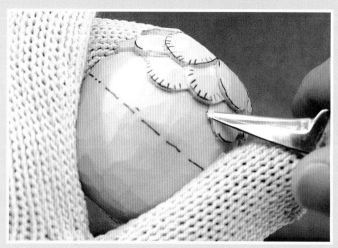

9 Carefully round the edges of the scales, paying particular attention to the grain of the wood.

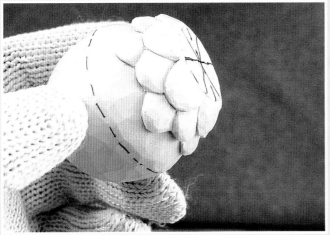

10 Compare your carving to the one in this photo. Are each of the scales defined on your piece?

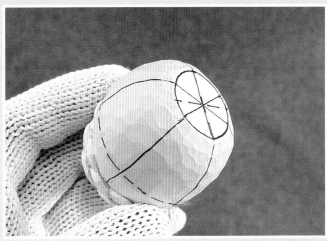

11 Make sure the ball is still evenly rounded top to bottom. Use a #3 ⅞" gouge and a detail knife to re-round as necessary. Draw vertical lines from the top to the scales, dividing the ball into six equal sections, as shown.

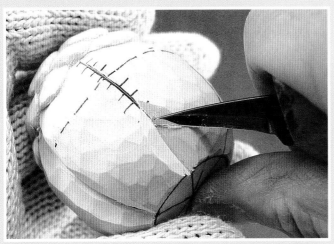

12 Using a bench knife, score these lines deeply and remove wood from both sides of the line, creating a deep trench.

13 You may want to use a V-tool to clean up the trench. If you do not have a V-tool, continue to use the bench knife to clean up the trench area. The V-tool just makes it a little faster and easier.

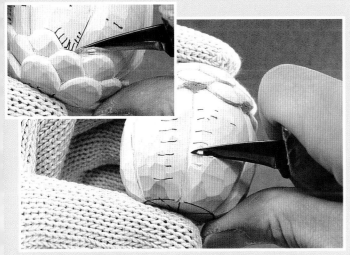

14 Round the areas around the trenches. Score the inner angles of the last row of scales with a detail knife to blend the trench lines under the scales. The finished ball should be rounded with rows of well-defined scales.

Applying What You've Learned

Once you know how to divide a ball into rounded vertical sections to make segments, you can create a number of different projects. The rounded sections of the pumpkins pictured here are examples of this technique. It can also be used to make flower petals.

block 8 scallops

Objective: Increase Carving Confidence

This block will give you more practice with carving angled sides. Additionally,

you will carve a decorative scalloped design using tools you are already familiar

with. As your carving confidence level increases, so will your own creativity. You

will now gain a sense of how these particular skills could be applied to future

carving projects.

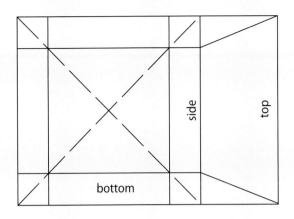

side

top

bottom

enlarge patterns 154%

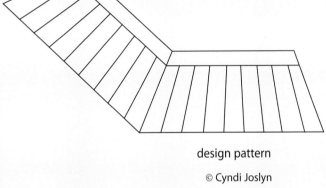

design pattern

© Cyndi Joslyn

tools and supplies

3" x 3" x 1¼" basswood block

Graphite paper

Stylus

Ruler

#3 ⅝" gouge

#3 ⅞" gouge

Bench knife

Detail knife

#12 4 mm V-tool

Fine-grit sandpaper or emery board

1 Transfer the pattern to the top and sides of the block. Add shading to show areas where the wood will be removed.

2 Follow the process of carving angled sides as described in Block 2 on page 54.

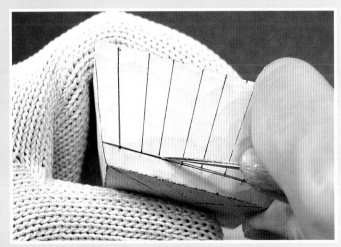

3 Transfer the design pattern to the sides of the block. Score the bottom line using a detail knife or a bench knife.

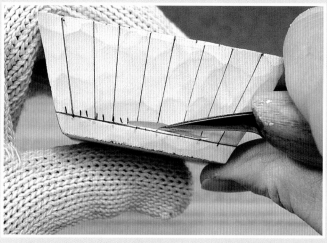

4 Remove a small amount of wood above the line, as shown.

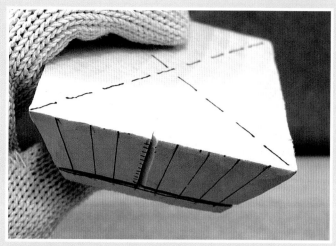

5 Score all of the vertical lines with a detail knife, and carve back to these lines, forming narrow trenches similar to the trenches carved on Block 7, page 74.

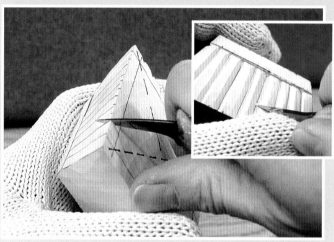

6 Use the detail knife to continue the scored lines to the top of the block. Then, deepen these lines with the detail knife.

7 Use a #3 ⅝" gouge to round and shape the narrow columns.

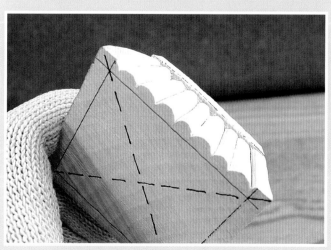

8 Refine the scalloped edge using a detail knife.

9 Don't forget to round the corner columns. Use the #12 4 mm V-tool to clean up the trenches. You can use a detail knife if you don't have #12 4 mm V-tool.

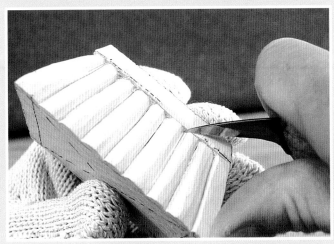

10 Round the edge of the bottom horizontal band using the detail knife, as shown.

11 Use the #3 ⅞" gouge to shave off the saw marks on the top and bottom of the block. On the bottom of the block only, draw lines connecting the opposite corners and reestablish the center point.

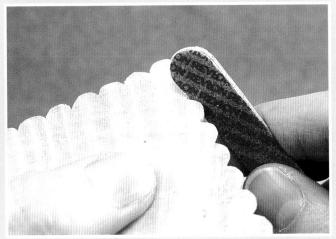

12 Use fine-grit sandpaper or an emery board to soften the scalloped edge.

13 Note the evenly scalloped edges on the finished angled block.

Applying What You've Learned

After you have learned to carve scallops, you can decorate many different pieces. The trim on Santa's apron is an example of this design.

Objective: Carving Lines and Leaf Designs

While carving Block 1 (see page 50), you learned how to create a cylinder with

evenly rounded sides. As you continue adding detail to Block 1 for this project,

you will gain more experience using a gouge. In addition, the exercise gives

you the opportunity to practice carving narrow, even lines with your detail

knife. Next, you will learn how to transfer and carve a lovely leaf design on that

cylinder, adding yet another element to your carving skills.

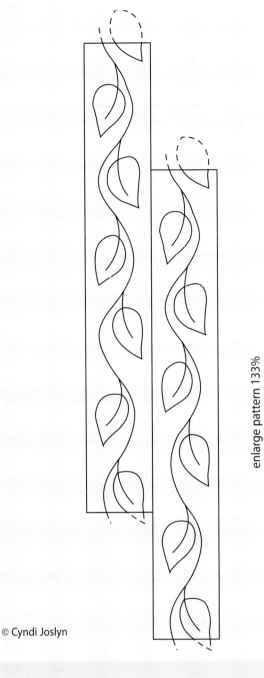

enlarge pattern 133%

© Cyndi Joslyn

tools and supplies

Block 1

Graphite paper

Stylus

Ruler

Extra-fine-point marker

#3 ⅞" gouge or #3 ⅝" gouge

Detail knife

1 Draw in ¼" borders at the top and bottom of the block (Block 1). Divide each ¼" border band into 1" segments followed by ½" segments. Score both horizontal border lines with a detail knife. Add shading in areas where the wood will be removed.

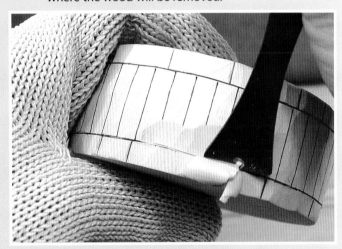

2 Use a #3 ⅝" gouge to remove the wood in this area.

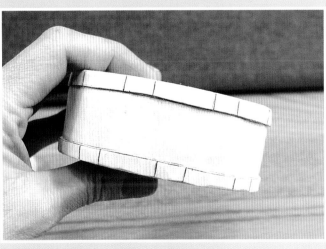

3 The wood removal creates a slight recess.

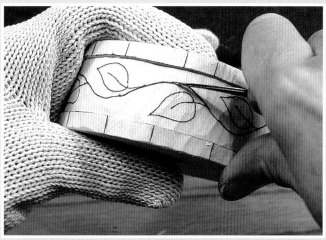

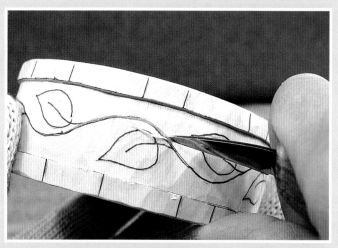

4 Transfer the leaf pattern to the sides of the cylinder, as shown. Retrace the transferred lines with an extra-fine-point marker. Score all of the lines with the detail knife.

5 With the detail knife, carve very thin, angled wedges from each side of the pattern line. A good rule of thumb for the correct size of this line is to carve away the width of the line made by the marker.

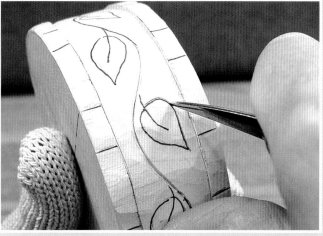

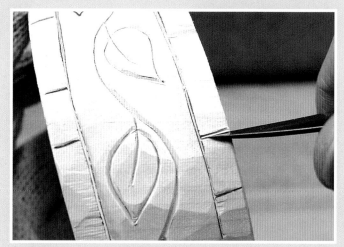

6 Continue to remove very thin wedges from both sides of the pattern lines on the leaves and veins of the leaves, as shown.

7 Score the vertical lines on the border bands. Remove thin wedges from either side of these vertical lines.

8 Round the sharp edges on the border bands.

9 The finished block shows a smooth recessed area with nicely scrolling leaves and vines.

Applying What You've Learned

Adding detail to a cylinder by using the incised technique of carving narrow, even lines with your detail knife is a technique frequently used to carve letters. Here it was used to define the different blocks of the quilt.

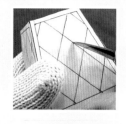

Objective: Rounding a Diamond Shape

This exercise builds upon the skills you learned in Block 2 (see page 54), where you carved flat, even, angled sides. Now, on that same block, you will add a quilted border design and practice the detailed rounding on diamond shapes to give it a puffy quilt effect. It's not as complicated as you might think and adds another interesting dimension to your carvings.

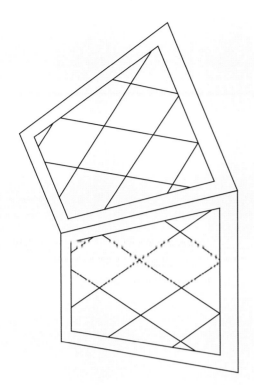

enlarge pattern 133%

© Cyndi Joslyn

tools and supplies

Block 2

Graphite paper

Stylus

Ruler

Bench knife

Detail knife

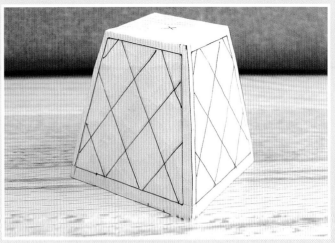

1 Transfer the design pattern to the sides of Block 2.

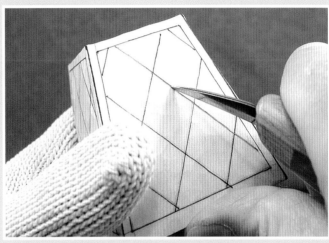

2 Score all of the lines with a detail knife.

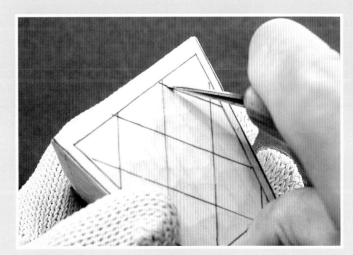

3 Score out from the narrow border bands to ensure the depth of the diagonal lines.

4 With a bench knife, remove a thin wedge of wood from both sides of all of the diagonal lines.

5 Remove a thin wedge of wood on the inside of all of the narrow border bands, as shown.

6 Using the detail knife, evenly round each diamond.

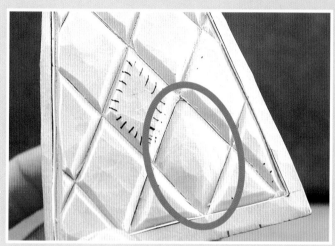

7 Rescore the diamond and deepen the design to create a puffed, or quilted, effect. Repeat this procedure on all four sides.

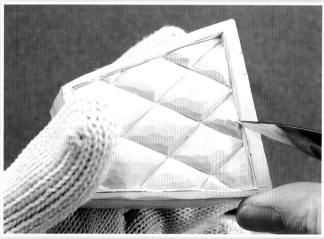

8 Round the sharp edges on all of the narrow borders.

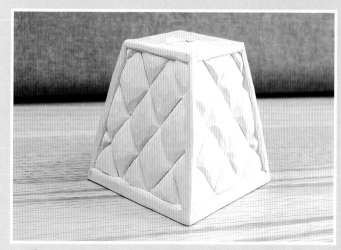

9 The finished block has a beautiful quilted look.

Applying What You've Learned

Use your new "quilting" skills to add texture and interest to unadorned borders. With or without a colorful paint finish, these lively and detailed accents will be sure to get attention!

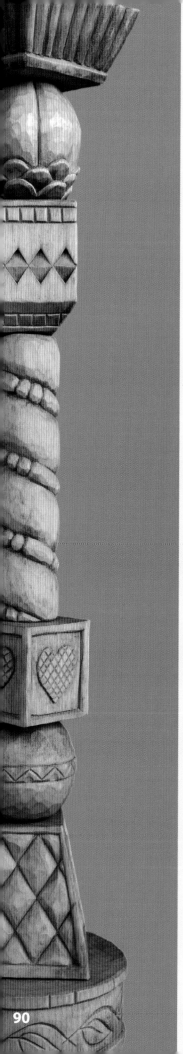

using your practice blocks

Objective: Putting it all Together

Congratulations! At this point you should have completed each of the practice blocks and gained many new carving skills. Now, you can put those blocks to good use. Here are some ideas to consider:

1 Keep them in your workspace to remind you how to do certain skills.

2 Use them individually to decorate your house or to give away as gifts. For example, Block 8 makes a beautiful votive candle holder. Drill a hole in the top of Block 7 and you have a gorgeous base for a taper candle. Block 4 makes an excellent gift for a loved one. (Now that you have the skills, you could even change that heart to a letter and make a handcarved baby shower gift!) Block 6 can easily keep the napkins on your picnic table from blowing away. You'll notice in the sidebars throughout the block projects that I've given you a variety of ideas for the ways you can use that block or skill. The possibilities of each of these blocks on their own is endless!

3 Join them together to build a beautiful candlestick. (I'll give you some instructions on that choice in a minute.)

After you decide how you are going to use your blocks, you need to decide how you want to finish them. Whether you decide to paint, stain, or wax the blocks is entirely up to you. Considering how they will be used will give you a good starting place for making your decision.

If your block will be purely decorative, try painting it. If you've used a wood that has a pretty grain, like butternut, think about using an oil finish. If your block will be handled a lot, use a varnished finish over the paint or paste wax over the oil finish.

Creating a candlestick

I decided to join my blocks together to create a unique candlestick. I chose this candlestick because I wanted a project that would use all of the individual blocks. As you become more familiar with carving, you may see other ways to combine individual blocks. Just as quilters may work together on separate squares of fabric that are then joined to create a quilt, some carving clubs ask each carver to create a block that is then joined with the other blocks in a "friendship cane." Relief carvers often create relief-carved quilts where each carver in the group creates one panel that is then joined into a large display.

tools and supplies

¼" drill bit and drill press or hand drill

16¼" length of ¼" dowel

Drafting square or contractor's square

Quick grip all-purpose adhesive

To finish the blocks for my candlestick, I decided to use a stain finish. However, depending on your mood or your personal preferences, this candlestick can be finished in a variety of ways, each one as delightful as the next.

You can finish each block individually before you assemble the candlestick, or you can assemble it first and finish them all at once as one completed candlestick. Whichever way you choose, be sure to refer to the finishing section on page 42 for more detailed information on methods and options.

Another thing to consider is how you want to assemble your candlestick. The one pictured here was assembled as we carved them, with Block 1 as the base and then building upward with each lesson. However, you may decide that you would like them assembled in a different order, and that's okay too. Just make sure the base is sturdy so that it will not tip over easily.

If you are making several candlesticks and want them to each take on a slightly different look, try mixing up the assembly sequence for each one. Leave out a block or two and create a grouping of candlesticks in staggered sizes. You may be surprised at just how different they will appear. However you decide to complete the project, you can take great pride in knowing that this is your very first handcarved item.

The instructions for joining all the blocks together to form a candlestick follow.

1 Use a ¼" drill bit to drill holes through Blocks 2 through 7 at the center points. Drill holes ½" deep in the top of Block 1 and in the bottom of Block 8. A drill press is easiest to use, but a hand drill used with care will suffice. Make the holes perpendicular to the blocks so the finished candlestick is straight.

2 Cut a 16¼" length of ¼" dowel. Insert the dowel into the hole in Block 1.

3 Verify with a square that the dowel is perpendicular to the top of Block 1. The dowel must be perpendicular for the candlestick to be straight.

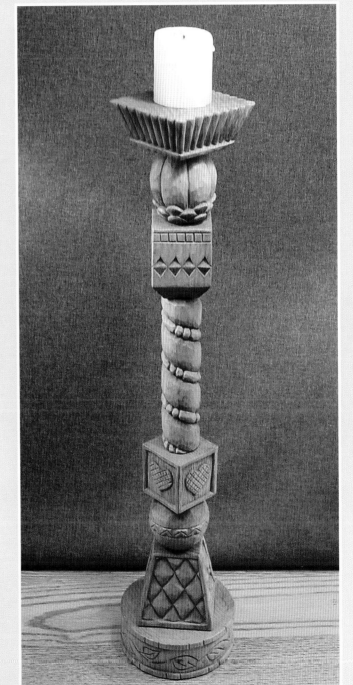

4 Dry fit all of the remaining blocks onto the dowel. Adjust the angles of the blocks to your liking. Remove the blocks and rethread them onto the dowel, gluing them as you go. You may want to make subtle registration marks on the blocks as you dry fit them. Then, when you glue them, they will be positioned exactly as you want them.

projects

All of the remaining projects presented in this book expand upon the carving skills you already acquired while working on the practice blocks. In addition, you will be shown new techniques. So before you go further, if you are not sure about a specific carving technique, refer back to that particular block to refresh your memory. You may even want to carve more blocks to practice that technique.

I wrote this book in such a way that all of the additional projects listed here give you, the beginning carver, more experience and add to your carving skills. To that end, they progressively increase in difficulty. So work at your own speed and have fun as you experience the joy of carving.

project 1 aztec angels

These delightful *Aztec Angels* make great pins or ornaments. One of the reasons that I included this project is so that you could learn the skill of scroll sawing. Each angel shape can be scroll sawn from a thin piece of basswood. If you don't have a scroll saw, you can buy precut shapes, cut them out using a coping saw, or use a gouge and knife to carve the cutout from the piece of wood by hand. This project also gives you more experience carving with the V-tool, which you will use to create the traditional Aztec designs on the angels.

A variety of patterns, colors, and embellishments lend infinite possibilities to this project.

tools and supplies

carving
• ⅜" x 3" x 4" basswood for each angel
• Stylus
• Graphite paper
• Detail knife
• #3 ⅞" or #3 ⅝" gouge
• 1 mm V-tool

painting
• #2, #6, #8 shader paintbrushes, such as Loew-Cornell Series #7300
• ¾" wash brush, such as Loew-Cornell Series #4550
• #1 liner brush, such as Loew-Cornell Series #7350
• 2 oz. bottles of acrylic paint in the following colors (I used Delta Ceramcoat):
    Light ivory
    Metallic copper
    Pumpkin
    Opaque yellow
    Magenta
    Passion
    Lima green
    Tompte red
    Azure blue

finishing
• Water-based satin interior varnish, such as Delta Ceramcoat

antiquing
• Antiquing medium and retarder, such as Jo Sonja's
• Dark flesh acrylic paint
• Worn-out flat brush
• Old rags
• Cotton swabs
• Antiquing solution is made with Antiquing medium and retarder, 1 part Dark flesh acrylic paint, 1 part

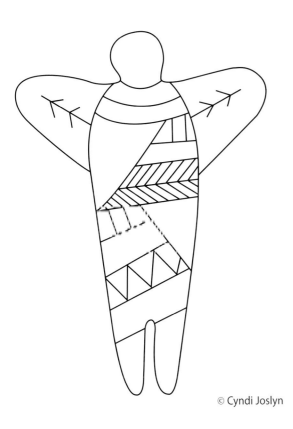

© Cyndi Joslyn

skills checklist

✔ Photocopy transfer, page 34

✔ Holding a gouge, page 5

✔ Holding a knife, page 3

✔ Pull cut, page 39

✔ Push cut, page 39

✔ Painting, page 42

practice blocks

Revisit this practice block	if you need practice with this skill
Block 1: Round Shapes	using a gouge
Block 3: Ball	using a knife
Block 4: Low Relief Carving	using a V-tool

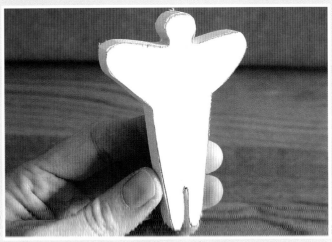

1 Choose a precut shape or start by transferring the pattern onto the wood (see the pattern to the left). If you don't have a precut shape, cut out the angel with scroll saw, a coping saw, or a knife and a gouge.

2 Using a detail knife, carve away the saw marks on the edges. Be mindful of how the grain changes as you carve. If you find the wood pulling or breaking, carve in the opposite direction to carve with the grain. Because I am making a pin, I carved just one side. If you are doing an ornament, you may wish to carve both sides.

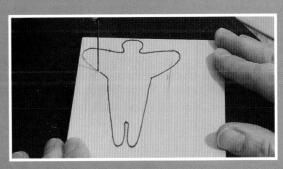

Using a Scroll Saw to Cut Shapes

Start by transferring the pattern to the wood. Then, insert and check your scroll saw blade. I would suggest a #3 skip tooth or reverse skip tooth blade for this project. If you have a scroll saw that accepts pin blades, these work fine also. Using both hands to guide the wood, carefully cut along the pattern lines with the scroll saw blade. Care should be taken when making very tight curves, and always be aware of where your hands are in relation to the moving blade. Be sure to wear protective eyewear when using power tools.

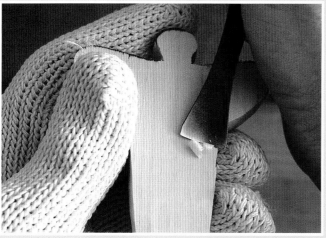

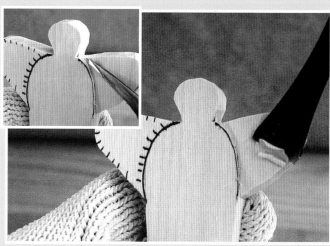

3 Using a #3 ⅝" gouge, shave off a thin layer of wood on the front of the angel. Remove all sawed or planed surfaces so the surface is covered with carved facets.

4 Transfer the line separating the body and the wings to the angel. Score this line with a detail knife and begin removing the wood in the shaded area. Continue to shape the wings with the #3 ⅝" gouge and the detail knife.

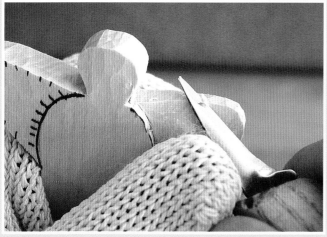

5 Round the wing edges with the detail knife. Then, transfer the pattern lines onto the wings.

6 Using a 1 mm V-tool, carve the pattern lines on the wings. Transfer the design lines to the body of the angel. Round the angel's head, as shown.

7 With the 1 mm V-tool, carve all of the design lines on the body.

8 Transfer the texturing lines to the various segments of the design. Then, V-tool the texture lines.

9 Carve away the sharp edges on the angel using the detail knife.

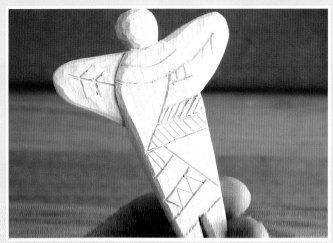

10 The finished angel has carefully rounded edges and a clearly incised design.

COLOR CHART

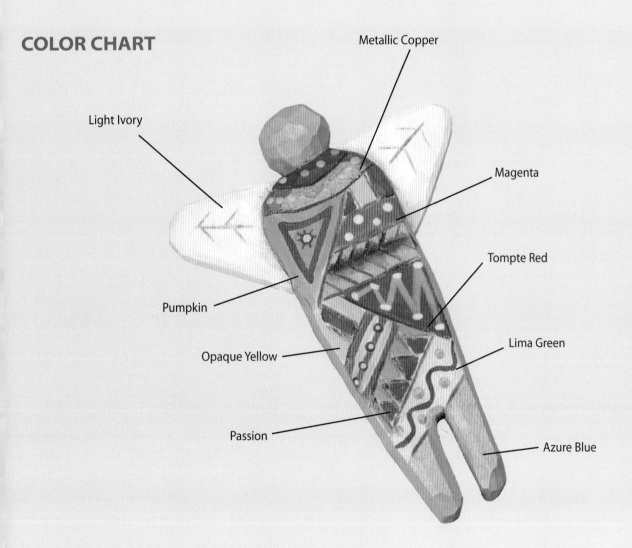

Light Ivory

Metallic Copper

Magenta

Pumpkin

Tompte Red

Opaque Yellow

Lima Green

Passion

Azure Blue

Antique with Dark Flesh.

project 2 bunny box

Incorporating a few more carving techniques, this project is a bit more difficult than the *Aztec Angels*. It also illustrates a simple way to embellish a manufactured box. I chose this project because carved boxes are so popular and there are all kinds of uses for them. Hopefully, after completing your first *Bunny Box*, your creative juices will kick in and inspire you to develop other handcarved designs for wooden boxes.

I chose to use my scroll saw to cut out the two bunnies and the flower on the top of this box. If you don't own a scroll saw, simply purchase several precut shapes at your local craft store or online. If you use cutouts, make sure they are made of wood, not plywood. When you transfer the pattern for the box top, substitute your bunny and flower cutouts for the ones I've included on the pattern.

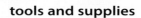

tools and supplies

carving
- 8" x 5¼" x 3" purchased basswood box (I used Walnut Hollow #1253OP)
- ⅜" x 3" x 10" piece of basswood or precut bunny and flower shapes
- Graphite paper
- Stylus
- Transparent tape
- Clear flexible ruler
- Tag board or template plastic
- #3 ⅞" or #3 ⅝"gouge
- 1 mm V-tool
- #7 4 mm gouge
- Detail knife
- Quick grip all-purpose adhesive, such as the one from Beacon Adhesives

painting
- #2, #6, #8 shader paintbrushes, such as Loew-Cornell #7300
- ¾" wash brush, such as Loew-Cornell Series #4550
- 2 oz. bottles of acrylic paint in the following colors (I used Delta Ceramcoat):
   Santa Fe rose
   Moroccan red
   Black
   Opaque yellow (Americana)
   Jubilee green
   Light ivory
   Tompte red
   Pink frosting

finishing
- Water-based satin interior varnish, such as Delta Ceramcoat

antiquing
- Antiquing medium and retarder, such as Jo Sonja's
- Brown iron oxide acrylic paint
- Worn-out flat brush
- Old rags
- Cotton swabs
- Antiquing solution is made with
   Antiquing medium and retarder, 1 part
   Brown iron oxide acrylic paint, 1 part

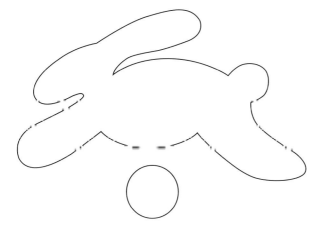

enlarge patterns 133%

© Cyndi Joslyn

templates

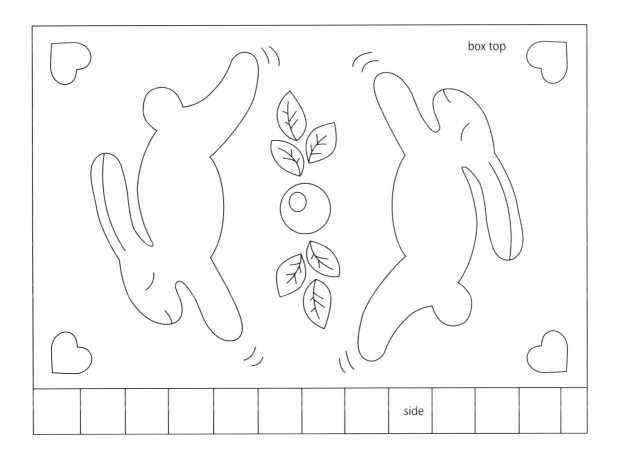

box top

side

skills checklist

✔ Photocopy transfer, page 35

✔ Using the pattern as a guide, page 36

✔ Holding a gouge, page 5

✔ Holding a knife, page 3

✔ Holding a V-tool, page 6

✔ Pull cut, page 39

✔ Painting, page 42

practice blocks

Revisit this practice block	if you need practice with this skill
Block 1: Round Shapes	using a gouge
Block 2: Angled Sides	removing saw marks with a gouge
Block 3: Ball	using a knife
Block 4: Low Relief Carving	creating a recess around a shape using a V-tool
Block 5: Pillar	creating a cylinder

1 Shave off the sawed faces on all sides of the box with a #3 ⅞" gouge. This step gives the entire box the illusion of being handcarved.

2 Center the pattern on the box top and tape it in place. Use graphite paper to transfer the hearts and leaves, following the pattern lines exactly. Trace the bunnies and the flower slightly inside the pattern lines if you're scrolling the shapes. If you're using precut shapes, trace them instead. Remove the graphite paper. Then, place dots at each corner of the pattern and connect the points to form a border.

3 On the box top, measure up ¾" from the opening on the side. Draw the line around all sides of the box. On the box bottom, measure down 1⅜" from the opening on the side. Draw a line around all sides of the box. This creates ½" bands at the top and bottom of the box.

4 Starting on the side with hinges, divide the bands into ⅝" sections using a clear flexible ruler. The final section may be a bit longer than ⅝". Make sure there is an even number of sections on each band. If you end up with an odd number, divide the longer section in two sections to arrive at an even number.

5 Using a 1 mm V-tool, carve all of the straight lines on both of the border bands.

6 With the 1 mm V-tool, carve the outline and vein lines on each leaf and the motion lines under the bunnies' feet. The box will be painted later, so there is no need to worry about any remaining pattern lines showing on the finished project.

7 Score around each heart with the detail knife.

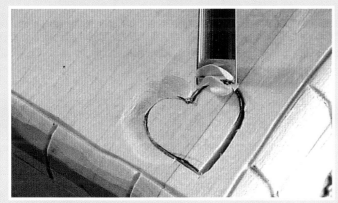

8 Using a #7 4 mm gouge, carve around each heart to add depth and highlight the heart. With the detail knife, carefully round the edges of the hearts.

9 If you're scrolling your own bunny and flower shapes, make templates of the bunny and flower patterns. Transfer the patterns to the ⅜" piece of basswood.

10 Using a scroll saw, cut out two bunnies and one flower or use precut shapes. Wood in the shaded area will be rounded with a detail knife.

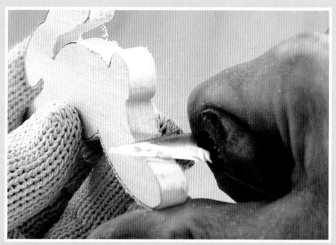

11 With the detail knife, carve away any saw marks on the edges of the bunnies and the flower.

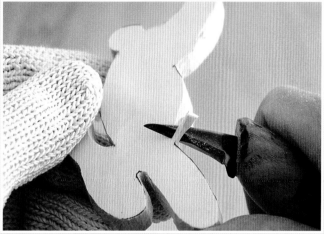

12 Use the detail knife to shape the body of the bunny.

13 Use #3 ⅝" gouge to further round and shape the bunnies and the flower.

14 Draw the details on the bunnies and carve them with a V-tool or the detail knife.

15 Glue the carved appliqués to the box using quick grip glue after the box and the appliqués have been painted.

16 The finished box top design features carefully incised designs and add-on appliqués. Remember that the painted appliqués will be glued to the box; then, the box will be varnished and antiqued.

COLOR CHART

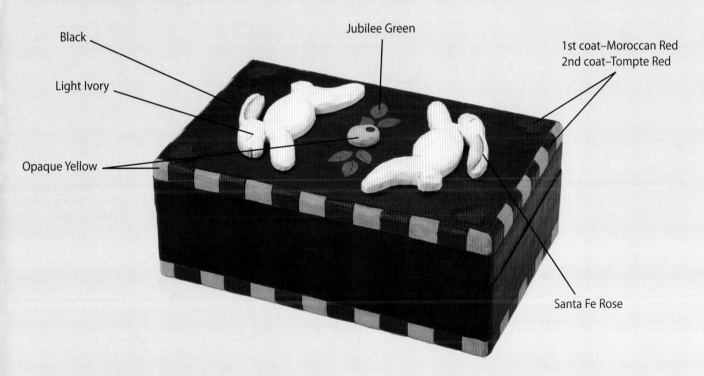

Black

Jubilee Green

1st coat–Moroccan Red
2nd coat–Tompte Red

Light Ivory

Opaque Yellow

Santa Fe Rose

Antique with Brown Iron Oxide.

project 3 snowman

I think everybody loves a snowman. There is just something about them that brings out the kid in each of us. Not only will you enjoy making him, you will also gain further experience carving evenly rounded shapes from a block of wood. The extra detailing on this project raises the difficulty level still higher. Remember, with each project, you are gaining more experience and becoming a better woodcarver.

tools and supplies

carving
- 2½" x 2½" x 7½" basswood block
- ½" x ½" x 1" basswood block
- 6" section of ¼" dowel
- Graphite paper
- Stylus
- #3 ⅝" gouge or #3 ⅞" gouge
- Bench knife
- Detail knife
- #5 3 mm gouge
- 1 mm V-tool
- Drill with ¼" bit
- Cyanoacrylate adhesive (instant glue)
- 2" length of baling wire
- Quick grip all-purpose adhesive, such as the one from Beacon Adhesives
- Manual drill with 1/16" bit

painting
- #2, #6, #8 shader paintbrushes, such as Loew-Cornell Series #7300
- ¾" wash brush, such as Loew-Cornell Series #4550
- #1 liner brush, such as Loew-Cornell Series #7350

- 2 oz. bottles of acrylic paint in the following colors (I used Delta Ceramcoat):
   Black
   Light ivory
   Purple
   Opaque yellow
   Tompte red
   Tangerine
   Jubilee green

antiquing
- Antiquing medium and retarder, such as Jo Sonja's
- Blue heaven acrylic paint
- Lima green acrylic paint
- Light ivory acrylic paint
- Worn-out flat brush
- Old rags
- Cotton swabs
- Antiquing solution is made with
   Antiquing medium and retarder, 7 parts
   Blue heaven acrylic paint, 4 parts
   Lima green acrylic paint, 1 part
   Light ivory acrylic paint, 2 parts

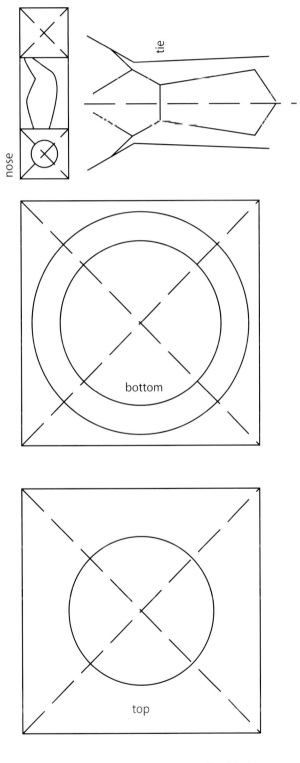

© Cyndi Joslyn

hat

brim

head

vest

enlarge pattern 133%

© Cyndi Joslyn

skills checklist

✔ Photocopy transfer, page 35

✔ Holding a knife, page 3

✔ Stop cut, page 38

✔ Pull cut, page 39

✔ Push cut, page 39

✔ Holding a gouge, page 5

✔ Wire doweling, page 47

✔ Painting, page 42

✔ Antiquing, page 44

1 Transfer the pattern to the wood. Add the shaded lines to show where the wood will be removed.

practice blocks	
Revisit this practice block	**if you need practice with this skill**
Block 1: Round Shapes	using a gouge
Block 2: Angled Sides	removing saw marks with a gouge
Block 3: Ball	using a knife
Block 4: Low Relief Carving	creating a recess around a shape using a V-tool
Block 5: Pillar	creating a cylinder

2 Score on the line with a bench knife, as shown.

3 Remove thin slices of wood with a #3 ⅞" gouge.

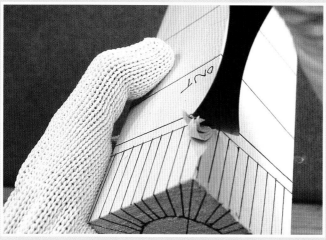

4 Use the gouge to rescore the line and release the thin slices of wood.

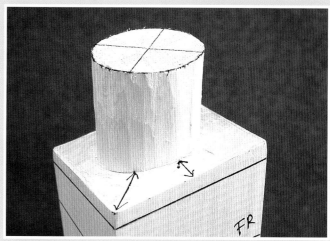

5 This will be the snowman's hat. Remember that more wood must be removed from the corners of the block than from the sides to achieve a truly round cylinder.

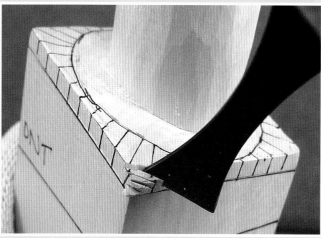

6 Measure out ⅜" from the base of the hat, creating a circle, as shown. The wood in the shaded area will be removed to create the brim of the snowman's hat. Score the line underneath the shaded area and remove the wood with a #3 ⅝" or a #3 ⅞" gouge.

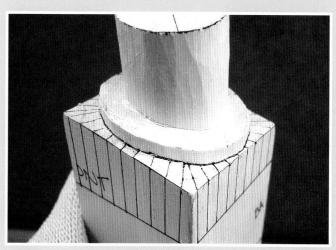

7 Add the lines for wood removal. Using a bench knife, score a line under the brim to a depth of ⅛". Then, remove the wood in the shaded area under the snowman's hat with a #3 ⅝" or a #3 ⅞" gouge to create a cylinder under the brim.

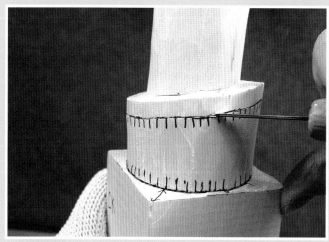

8 Rescore under the brim of the hat and at the base of the snowman's head with the bench knife to make these cuts deeper. Round the wood under the brim of the hat and at the base of the snowman's head.

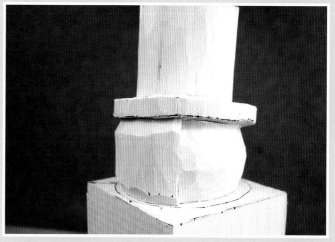

9 Continue rounding with the bench knife or the detail knife until the head is evenly rounded, as shown on the right side of the photo. The corner of the block to the base of the head should measure about ¾" deep.

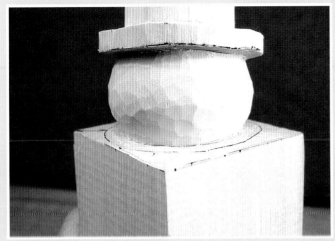

10 Both sides of the snowman's head are now evenly rounded.

11 On the bottom of the block, add shading lines to show the areas where the wood is to be removed.

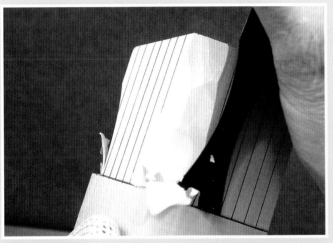

12 Score the horizontal line around the middle of the snowman (up about 2½" from the bottom of the block) with a bench knife. Use a #3 ⅞" gouge to carve back to the scored line.

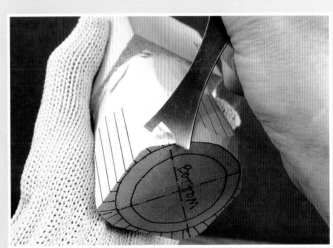

13 Continue to remove the wood with the #3 ⅞" gouge.

14 The block should now look like several cylinders, a ball, and a square joined together.

15 Draw lines from the corners to the head to establish the shoulders. This will be the snowman's vest.

16 Start at the bottom of the vest and round up to the snowman's neck and shoulders.

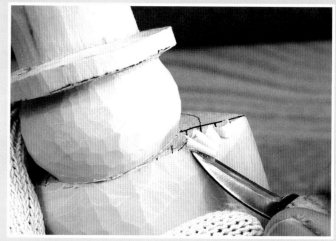

17 A bench knife is also helpful as you continue to round the shoulder area.

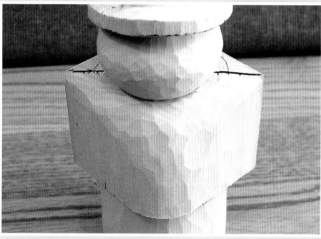

18 The rounding process on the front half of the snowman should match this model.

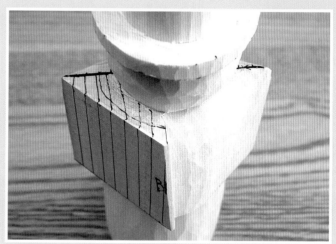

19 Repeat this rounding process on the back of the snowman's vest.

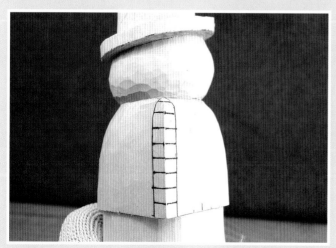

20 Draw a line ½" out from the corner edges on the front and back of the snowman.

21 Remove the wood in the shaded area with a #3 ⅞" gouge. This will be the armhole of the snowman's vest.

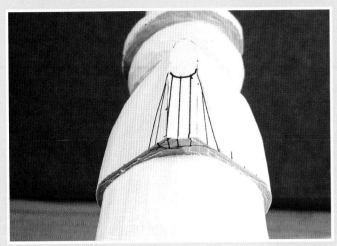

22 Draw in the bottom line of the armhole about ¾" down from the shoulder line. The wood in the shaded area will be removed.

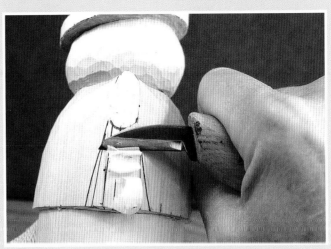

23 Round the shaded area under the armhole with a bench knife.

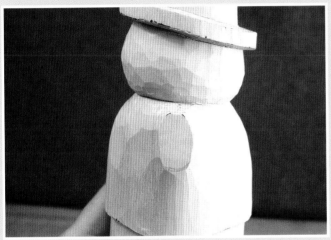

24 This photo shows the progress to this point.

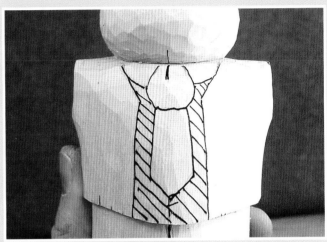

25 Draw or transfer the tie pattern to the front of the snowman.

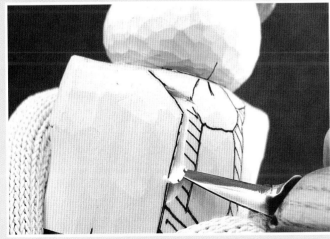

26 Score all the lines around the tie and remove the wood in the shaded area with a detail knife.

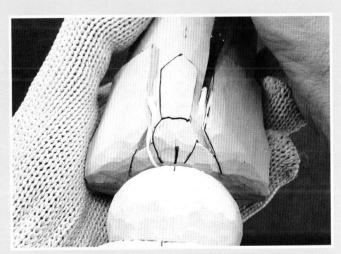

27 Use a #5 3 mm gouge to remove the wood in the narrow spaces between the tie and the vest.

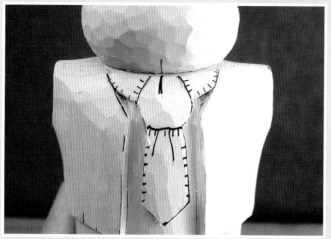

28 Using the detail knife, remove the wood in the shaded areas to begin shaping the tie.

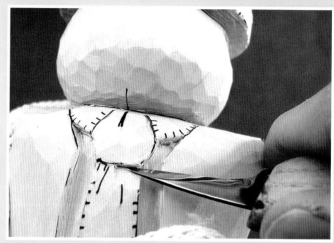

29 Round the edges of the tie and remove a small amount of wood under the knot of the tie.

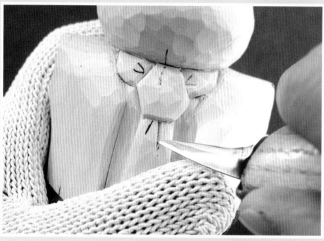

30 Score the crease lines under the knot and on both sides of the knot. Remove a thin slice of wood on both sides of the score lines to create the creases on the tie.

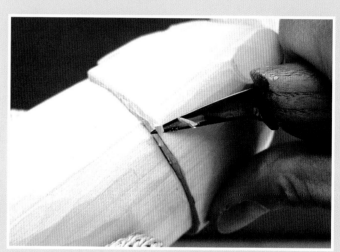

31 Round the edge of the vest with a detail knife.

32 Draw in some random patches on the vest and the hat like the ones shown.

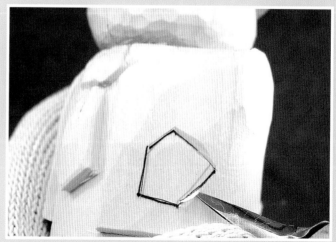

33 Use the detail knife to score around the patches and remove a small amount of wood outside the patch lines to define them.

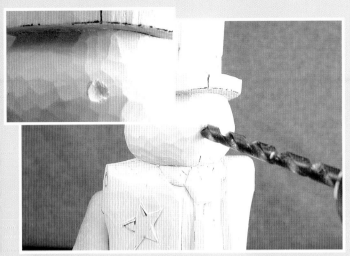

34 Using a ¼" drill bit, drill a slight indentation on the snowman's face to hold his carrot nose.

35 Continuing with the ¼" drill bit, drill holes approximately ½" deep to hold the dowels that will be the snowman's arms.

36 Cut two pieces of ¼" dowel 2¼" long. With a detail knife, round one end of each dowel. Dry fit the flat end of the dowels into the arm holes. Wait until the snowman is painted before affixing the arms to the body with quick grip adhesive.

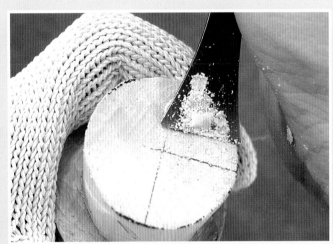

37 With the #3 ⅝" or the #3 ⅞" gouge, shave off the saw marks on the top of the snowman's hat.

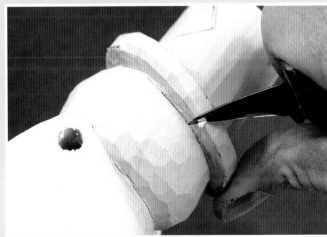

38 With a detail knife, round the sharp edges on the hat top and on the brim.

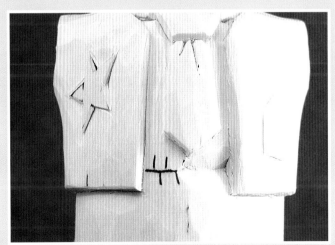

39 Draw a horizontal line near the bottom edge of the vest front, as shown. Use the detail knife to score this line and carve back to both sides of this line, creating a slight trench to define the snowman's waist.

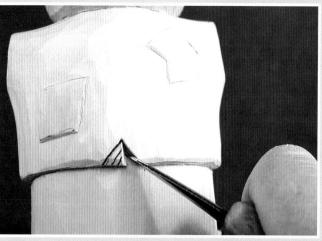

40 Add further detail to the back of the vest by drawing a triangle with a ⅜" base at the center of the back of the vest, as shown. Score these lines and remove the wedge of wood inside the triangle.

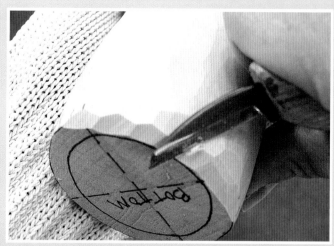

41 Round the bottom of the snowman to the inside circle.

42 Transfer the pattern to the ends of the ½" x ½" x 1" piece of wood. This will be the snowman's carrot nose. Remove the wood outside of the circle.

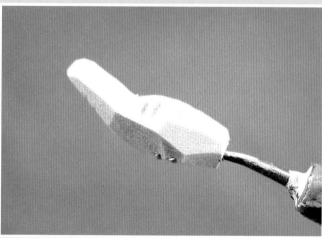

43 Continue to carve a carrot shape, as shown. Add a few detail lines around the carrot with a 1 mm V-tool. Use a fine-point stylus or a manual drill and a ⅟₁₆" bit to drill a hole in the end of the carrot nose. Glue a ½" length of baling wire in this hole with cyanoacrylate (CA) glue.

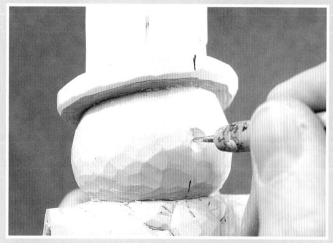

44 Add a corresponding hole in the indentation of the snowman's face. Dry fit the nose, but do not glue it yet.

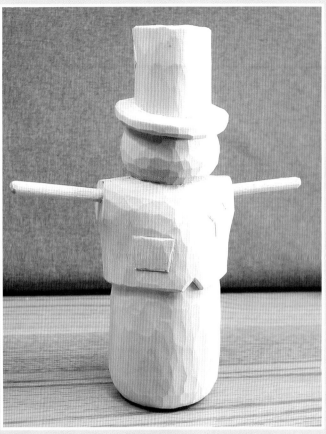

45 The front of the snowman with the nose in place will look like this. After the snowman is painted, wire dowel the nose to the snowman's face using CA glue.

46 A view of the snowman's back.

COLOR CHART

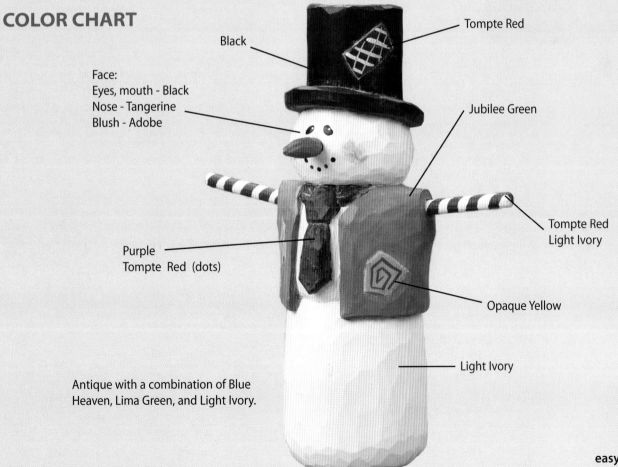

Black

Tompte Red

Face:
Eyes, mouth - Black
Nose - Tangerine
Blush - Adobe

Jubilee Green

Tompte Red
Light Ivory

Purple
Tompte Red (dots)

Opaque Yellow

Light Ivory

Antique with a combination of Blue
Heaven, Lima Green, and Light Ivory.

project 4 cypress knee santa

Cypress knees are tuberous growths that form on the roots of mature cypress trees. I discovered them one day while watching television. Someone was painting one, and I wondered how it would be to carve. I didn't know if they would be as hard as iron, which was a distinct possibility. Eventually my curiosity got the best of me. I purchased a cypress knee on eBay and was surprised by how soft and easy it was to carve. Since then, I've had a lot of fun with them and thought you might, too.

Cypress knees are available commercially in their natural state (bark on) or peeled and cleaned. I have found cypress knees ranging in size from 4 inches to 36 inches. Starting with a peeled and cleaned cypress knee allows me to get to the fun part faster. Either way, using a cypress knee will give you experience carving on "found wood." Santas are particularly dear to my heart. That is why I chose Santa as the subject of this project.

Every cypress knee is different, so each Santa you carve will be unique. But this technique can be adapted to any cypress knee. The only carving tool you will need for this project is a detail knife.

tools and supplies

carving
- Peeled and cleaned cypress knee
- Pencil or marker
- Detail knife

painting
- #2, #6, #8 shader paintbrushes, such as, Loew-Cornell Series #7300
- ¾" wash brush, such as Loew-Cornell Series #4550
- # 1 liner brush, such as Loew-Cornell Series #7350
- Stylus
- 2 oz. bottles of acrylic paint in the following colors (I used Delta Ceramcoat):
    Medium flesh
    Adobe red
    Light ivory
    Black cherry
    Maroon
    Black
    Hunter green
    Chocolate cherry
    Metallic gold
    Autumn brown (for brown eyes)
    Blue haze (for blue eyes)

finishing
- Satin interior varnish, such as Delta Ceramcoat

antiquing
- Antiquing medium and retarder, such as Jo Sonja's
- Raw sienna acrylic paint
- Burnt sienna acrylic paint
- Worn-out flat brush
- Old rags
- Cotton swabs
- Antiquing solution is made with
    Antiquing medium and retarder, 2 parts
    Raw sienna acrylic paint, 1 part
    Burnt sienna acrylic paint, 1 part

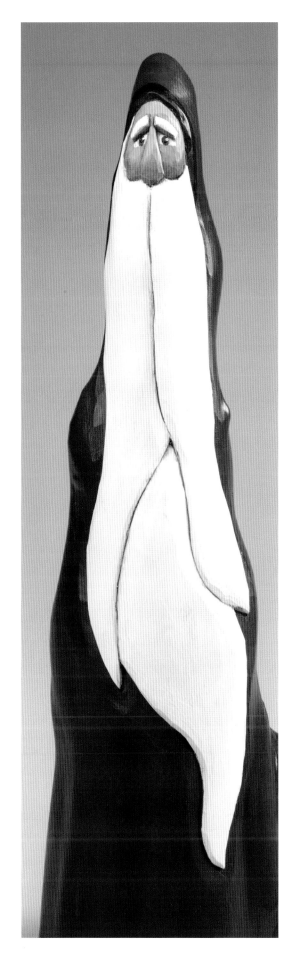

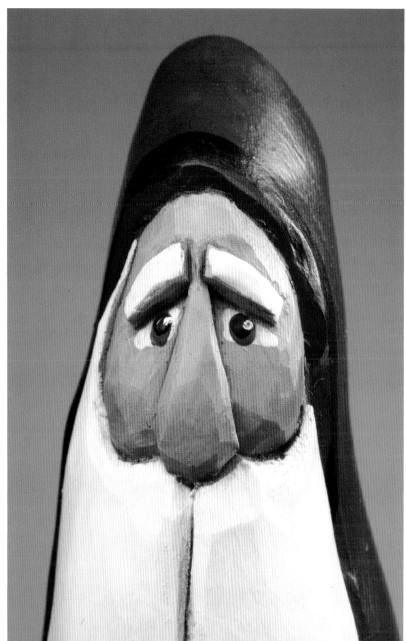

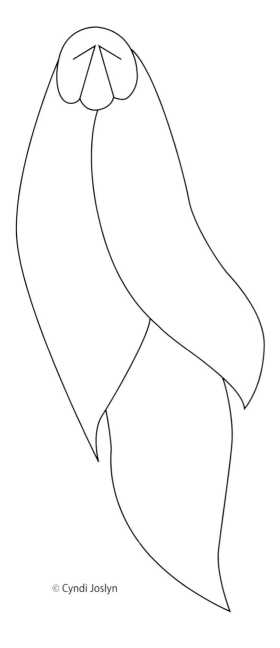

© Cyndi Joslyn

skills checklist

✔ Freehand transfer, page 37

✔ Holding a knife, page 3

✔ Stop cut, page 38

✔ Painting, page 42

✔ Antiquing, page 44

practice blocks	
Revisit this practice block	**if you need practice with this skill**
Block 3: Ball	using a knife
Block 5: Pillar	creating stop cuts

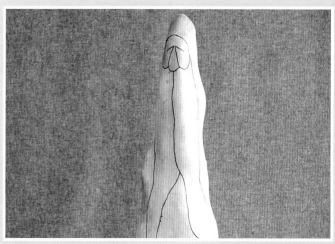

1 For this example, I am using a 12" cypress knee. Draw a face on the cypress knee with pencil. Your pattern lines should be as subtle as possible. I'm using marker in these photos for photographic clarity.

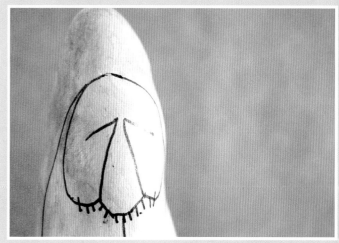

2 Add shading to show where the wood will be removed under the nose and cheeks.

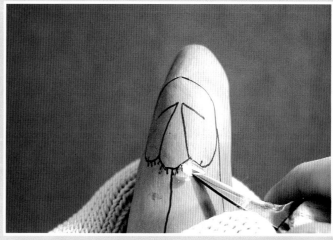

3 Score under the nose and cheek with a detail knife. Remove a small amount of the wood in the shaded area. Repeat each carving process on each side of the face.

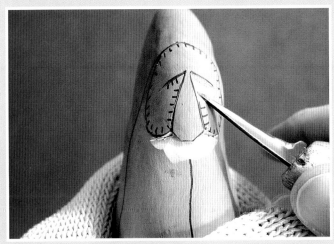

4 Score around all of the remaining face lines. Remove a small amount of the wood under the eyebrow, as shown.

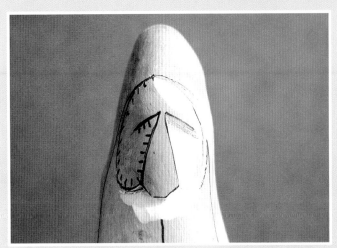

5 Continue to remove a small amount of wood on the side of Santa's nose. Shape the cheek area and remove the wood on the inside of the hood area.

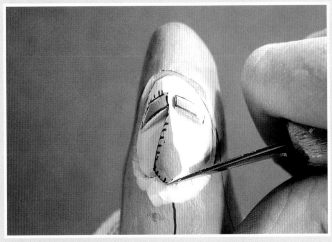

6 Draw the eyebrows. Score the eyebrow lines and remove a tiny amount of wood around them to give them definition.

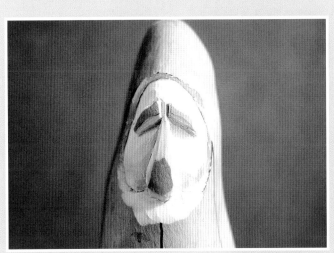

7 Round the edges of Santa's nose with the detail knife.

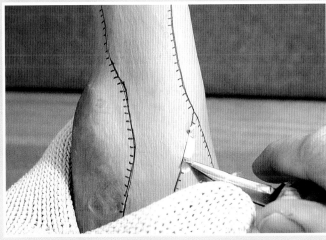

8 Add the lines to show wood removal around the mustache lines. Score the lines with the detail knife. Remove the wood in the shaded area below and around the mustache using the stop cutting technique.

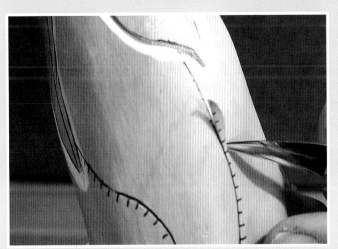

9 Add the shading to show wood removal around the beard. Then, score the lines around the beard and remove the wood in the shaded area.

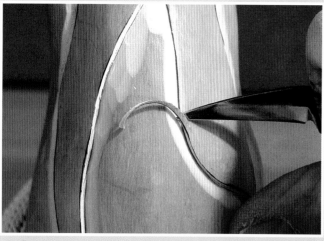

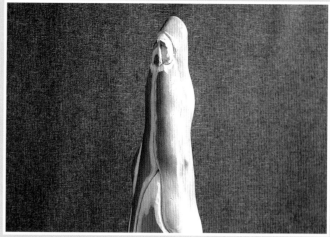

10 Shave off any sharp edges on the mustache and beard.

11 The carved Santa is simply composed of a series of stop cuts that define the features.

COLOR CHART

The *Cypress Knee Santa* is base coated with several very thin washes of paint. Washes are created by mixing one part paint with one part water. Allow washes to dry 15 minutes between coats.

First coat: Black cherry
Second coat: Maroon

After the base coats are dry, gently wipe the surface of the Santa with a damp, soft cloth, which will lift off some of the paint. Wipe the surface until the desired effect is achieved. Apply a wash of tompte red. Allow to dry.

Continue the process of applying washes and gently wiping the surface until the desired effect is achieved. Allow the Santa to dry completely, and then apply two coats of varnish according to the directions in the Painting and Finishing Techniques section on page 43.

Medium Flesh
Blush with Adobe

Light Ivory

Antique with a combination of
Raw Sienna and Burnt Sienna.

Black

Do-dad border

Measure up ¼" from the bottom of the Santa and draw a line around the base. Measure up ⅝" from the bottom of the Santa and draw a second line around the base. This creates a ⅜" border. Paint the border black. With a liner brush, add thin lines of black above and below border band. Allow to dry.

1. With a wooden paintbrush, dip the end into maroon paint. Touch the end of the paintbrush to where you want the dot. Redip for each dot to keep the dots consistent in size.

2. With the liner brush, add leaves of hunter green.

3. With the stylus, add dots of chocolate cherry.

4. With a stylus, add dots of metallic gold.

Tips for painting faces

When painting the *Cypress Knee Santa*, paint the body first, then the face, and finally the beard. Base coat the face with two coats of medium flesh. Blush the cheeks with adobe. It's okay if the blush strays into the beard area. Make sure to get the paint well into all of the creases under the Santa's cheeks and nose.

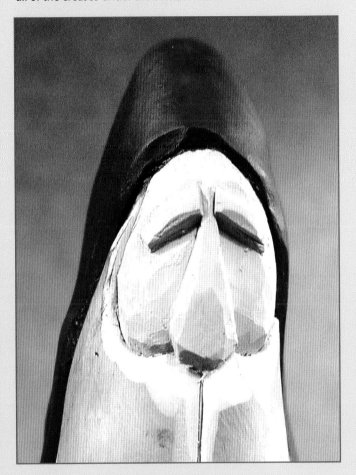 

Tips for painting eyes

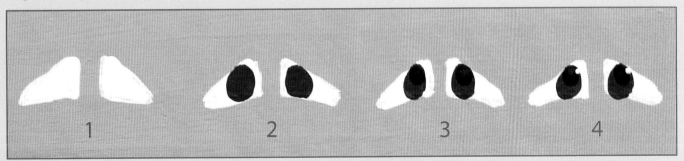

1. With a liner brush, paint in triangles of light ivory for the whites of the eyes. The outside corner of the eye should be lower than the inside corner.

2. Again with the liner brush, add the iris color. I like autumn brown for brown eyes, blue haze for blue eyes.

3. With the liner brush, add black pupils.

4. Finish with sparkles of light ivory added with a fine-pointed stylus. Sparkles should be on the right side of the right eye and the right side of the left eye.

project 5 shell paperweight

I chose the *Shell Paperweight* project to give you the opportunity to carve on yet another type of wood—butternut. Like basswood, butternut is a superior wood for intricate carving. But unlike basswood, it possesses a beautiful color and rich grain pattern that offers you more finishing options. This exercise also gives you experience carving woods with a visual wood grain. Don't let the grain sway you from the pattern lines.

tools and supplies

carving
- 1½" x 3" x 3" butternut block
- Graphite paper
- Stylus
- #3 ⅞" or #3 ⅝" gouge
- Bench knife
- Detail knife
- 1 mm V-tool
- ⅞" USS flat washer
- Quick grip all-purpose adhesive, such as the one from Beacon Adhesives
- 3" x 3" felt square
- Scissors

finishing
- Boiled linseed oil
- Worn-out flat brush
- Soft cloths

skills checklist

✔ Photocopy transfer, page 35

✔ Holding a knife, page 3

✔ Stop cut, page 38

✔ Pull cut, page 39

✔ Push cut, page 39

✔ Holding a gouge, page 5

✔ Finishing with oil, page 45

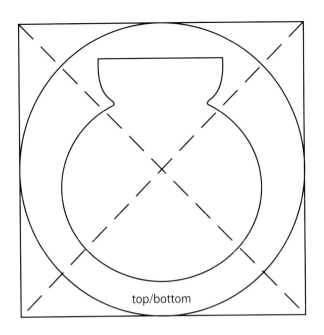

top/bottom

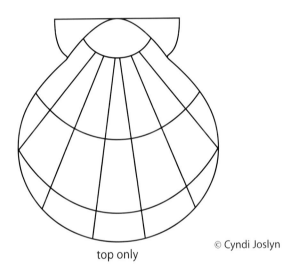

top only

© Cyndi Joslyn

practice blocks

Revisit this practice block	if you need practice with this skill
Block 1: Round Shapes	using a gouge
Block 3: Ball	using a knife
Block 8: Scallops	creating scallops
Block 1, Exercise 2: Incised Designs	creating a recessed area

1 Transfer or draw a 3" circle on the top and bottom of the block of wood, as shown. Add shading to show the wood that is to be removed.

2 Use a #3 ⅞" gouge to remove the wood from the shaded area. Working with butternut requires paying more attention to wood grain. Carve with the grain as much as possible.

3 Transfer the shell outline to the top of the cylinder. Measure up from the bottom of the cylinder ¾" and draw a line around the cylinder. Add shading to show where the wood will be removed.

4 Using a #3 ⅞" gouge, remove the wood in the shaded area outside the shell to the line around the cylinder.

5 Compare your carving with this example. Notice how flat the ledge is.

6 Transfer the shell pattern to the block. Mark the line endpoints on the sides of the shell.

7 Extend these lines to the base of the shell. This will enable you to reestablish the ray of lines after the shell is rounded. Shade the "wings" for wood removal, and then score the lines between the shell and the wings using a bench knife or a detail knife.

8 Remove the wood from the shaded area to ⅛", as shown.

9 Using a bench knife, round the shell. Continue to pay close attention to carving with the grain of the wood.

10 When the shell is evenly rounded, reestablish the shell pattern lines using the endpoint marks made in Step 6.

11 Score the horizontal curved lines with a detail knife.

12 Remove a small amount of wood under each line using the stop cutting technique.

13 Score all of the vertical lines up to the small shell cap near the wings. Remove wedges of wood on either side of these vertical lines, much in the same fashion we used on Block 8 (see page 78).

14 Repeat this process on the remaining two curved tiers of the shell.

15 Maintain the horizontal curved lines while you shape the vertical rays by recarving the horizontal edges as needed. Add three vein lines on the top wings with a 1 mm V-tool.

16 Draw a line ¼" up from the base of the cylinder. Score this line with a bench knife and remove a small amount of wood above the line in the shaded area.

17 With the bench knife, round the top and bottom edges, as shown by the shading.

18 Trace the outline of the washer on the bottom of the paperweight.

19 Score this line and begin removing the wood inside the circle with a detail knife.

20 Continue to remove the wood inside the circle to a depth of approximately ⅛". Switch to a #3 ⅞" gouge to complete this task.

21 This recess should be deep enough for the washer to fit flush with the bottom of the wood. When the recess is deep enough, glue the washer in place with quick grip adhesive.

22 Cut a piece of felt to cover the bottom of the paperweight. After the finish has been applied to the paperweight, glue the felt in place with quick grip adhesive.

23 The carved paperweight is ready for finishing. I used an oil finish (see the instructions on page 45).

project 6 welcome sign

This is the most complex project for transferring a pattern. Accurate placement of the pattern is going to determine to a great degree how well the project is executed. I designed this project to give you experience working on a larger-dimension relief carving. You will also have the opportunity to carve with a chisel and mallet. I used a mallet to outline the border and the letters on the *Welcome Sign*.

tools and supplies

carving
- 1" x 9" x 19" basswood board
- ⅜" x 4" x 7" piece of basswood for tree, moose, bear, and fish shapes (or precut shapes)
- Graphite paper
- Stylus
- #1 8 mm chisel (or 10 mm or 12 mm chisel)
- Mallet
- #3 ⅞" gouge or #3 ⅝" gouge
- #7 14 mm gouge
- Detail knife
- Bench knife
- Skew knife
- 22-gauge copper wire
- Small beads, various colors
- Needle-nose pliers
- Manual drill with ¹⁄₁₆" bit
- Cyanoacrylate glue

painting
- #2, #6, #8 shader paintbrushes, such as, Loew-Cornell Series #7300
- # 1 liner brush, such as Loew-Cornell Series #7350
- ¾" wash brush, such as Loew-Cornell Series #4550

- 2 oz. bottles of acrylic paint in the following colors (I used Delta Ceramcoat):
    Golden brown
    Barn red
    Maple sugar tan
    Black cherry
    Hunter green
    Brown iron oxide
    Western sunset yellow

finishing
- Water based satin interior varnish, such as Delta Ceramcoat or spar varnish (if the sign is used outside)

antiquing
- Antiquing medium and retarder, such as Jo Sonja's
- Spice brown acrylic paint
- Burnt sienna acrylic paint
- Worn-out flat brush
- Old rags
- Cotton swabs
- Antiquing solution is made with
    Antiquing medium and retarder, 2 parts
    Spice brown acrylic paint, 1 part
    Burnt sienna acrylic paint, 1 part

skills checklist

✔ Photocopy transfer, page 35

✔ Using the pattern as a guide, page 36

✔ Holding a knife, page 3

✔ Stop cut, page 38

✔ Pull cut, page 39

✔ Push cut, page 39

✔ Holding a gouge, page 5

✔ Using a mallet, page 7

✔ Wire doweling, page 47

✔ Painting, page 42

✔ Antiquing, page 44

practice blocks	
Revisit this practice block	**if you need practice with this skill**
Block 1: Round Shapes	using a gouge
Block 3: Ball	using a knife
Block 4: Low Relief Carving	using a V-tool
	creating a recess within a small border
Block 6: Chip Carving	using a skew knife
	making angled cuts
	creating even squares
Block 1, Exercise 2: Incised Designs	creating a recessed area

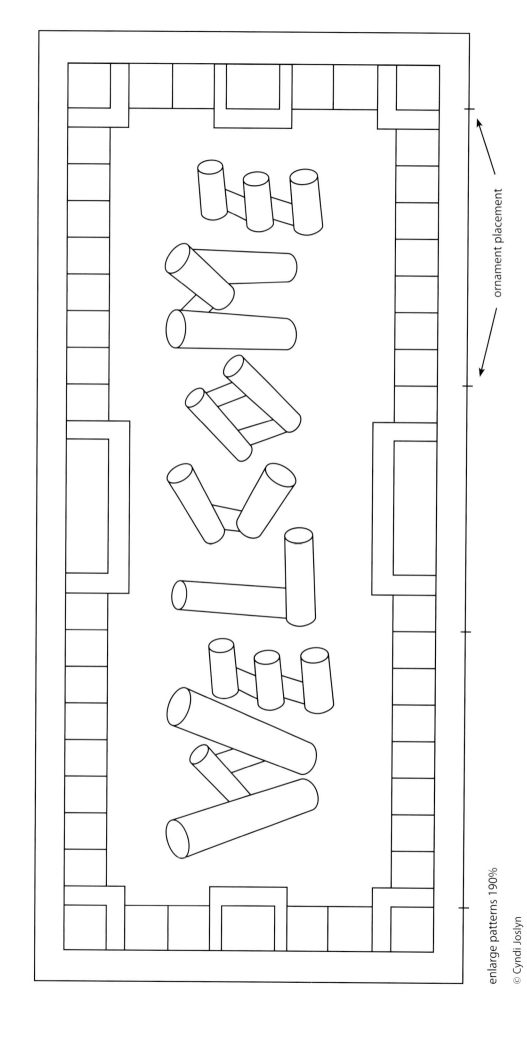

ornament placement

enlarge patterns 190%

© Cyndi Joslyn

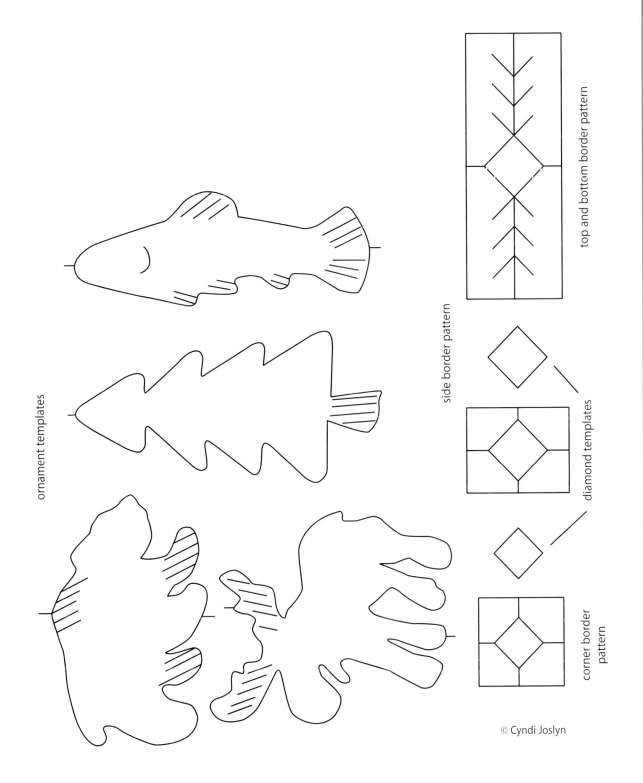

ornament templates

side border pattern

top and bottom border pattern

diamond templates

corner border pattern

© Cyndi Joslyn

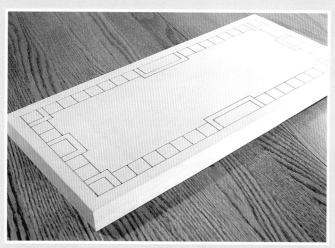

1 To get the best end product, be very careful when transferring the pattern. Make sure the outline border is centered. I draw this part on using the pattern as a guide, but I also use a ruler for accuracy. This helps me get straighter lines, more even borders, and a centered design.

2 Photocopy the pattern and cut out the inner "welcome" section. Tape it in place inside the border. Sandwich graphite paper between the pattern and the wood and transfer the pattern. This ensures accurate placement.

3 Using a #1 8 mm chisel and a mallet, outline all of the straight lines on the border to a depth of ⅛". If you would rather not use a mallet, this part of the project can be carved with a bench knife.

4 With a bench knife, score all of the straight lines on the "welcome" part of the sign.

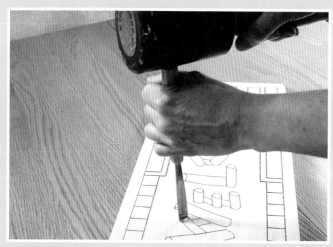

5 Use a #7 14 mm gouge and a mallet to create stop cuts for the ends of the letters. You can also create stop cuts for the ends of the letters with a detail knife.

6 With the #7 14 mm gouge, start to remove the wood around each letter. I like to use a #7 tool on this part of the project because it creates facets with a greater curved surface and accentuates the background of the project.

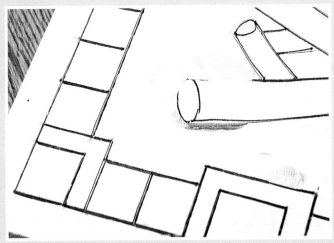

7 Remove the wood to about ⅛" deep.

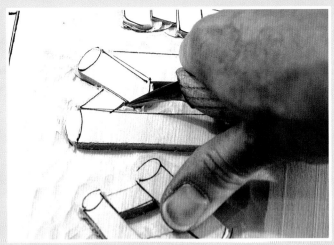

8 Use a detail knife to get into the tiny areas not accessible with the #7 14 mm gouge.

9 With the #7 14 mm gouge, start inside the right-hand border and begin to remove the background wood to a depth of ⅛".

10 Use a bench knife to remove long, thin slices of wood inside the border to a depth of ⅛". This will help you judge how much wood needs to be removed from the background.

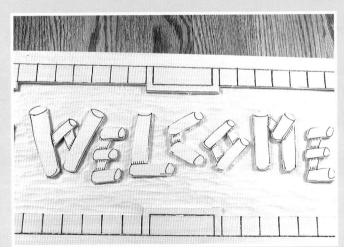

11 The letters consist of combinations of stacked logs. Use the shading in the above photo as a guide to begin preliminary wood removal: It will show you which logs tuck behind others.

12 With a #3 ⅝" gouge, remove the wood in the shaded areas to create various levels in the letters.

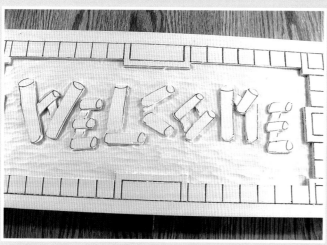

13 Compare your progress to this point with this photograph of the piece.

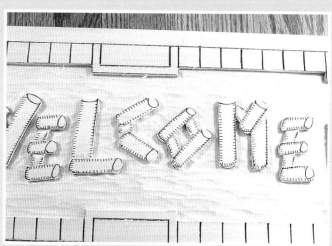

14 The shaded areas of letters will be rounded. Add lines to your piece to show where wood will be removed.

15 Use the detail knife to round all of the edges on the logs (refer to the shading in Step 14) except the ends of the logs with ovals.

16 Rescore around each letter and use a #3 ⅝" gouge to clean up and define each one.

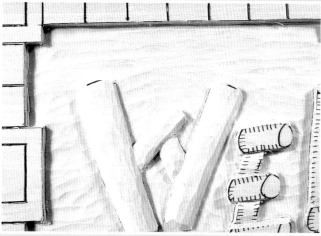

17 Notice the sharper definition after the *W* has been cleaned up.

18 Redraw the circles on the ends of the logs, as shown.

19 Use a detail knife to slice a flat, angled plane inside of each oval.

20 Remove a small amount of wood in the shaded area on the outside of the border blocks.

21 Use a bench knife to make an angled cut to a depth of about ⅛".

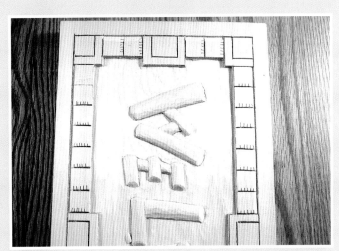

22 Mark the wood to be removed from the shaded area of the sides of each block, as shown.

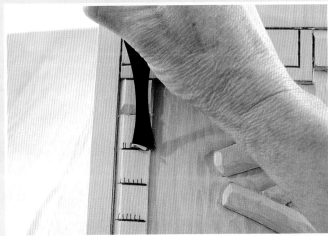

23 Use a #3 ⅝" gouge to remove the wood from the shaded areas.

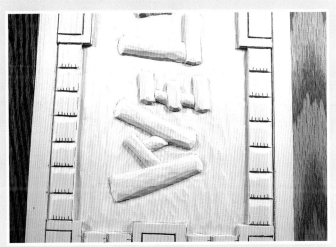

24 Remove a small amount of wood on the other sides of the blocks as well.

25 This photo shows the progress to this point.

26 Using a bench knife, carve away an angled slice on the inside edge of each block on the long sides of the border, as shown.

27 On the short sides of the border, use a #3 ⅝" gouge because you are dealing with cross-grain cuts.

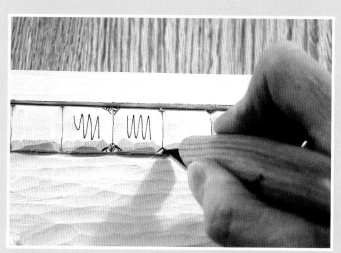

28 Using a skew knife, take tiny angled slices out of the corner of each block, as shown.

29 Use a #3 ⅝" gouge to shave a thin layer of wood off the top of each block.

30 Shade the rectangles and larger squares of the border for wood removal, as shown.

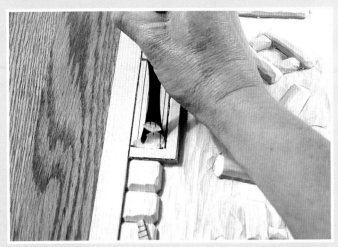

31 Score the inside border lines with a bench knife. Use a #3 ⅝" gouge to remove this wood.

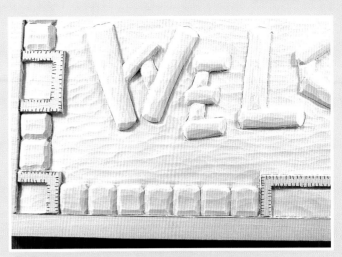

32 Shade the edges of the brackets, as shown.

33 With a detail knife, round both edges on all of the brackets.

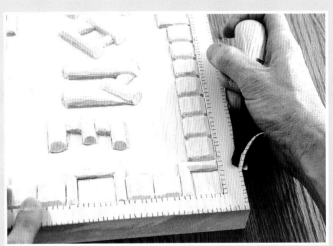

34 With a #3 ⅞" gouge, slightly round both edges of the frame that surrounds the sign.

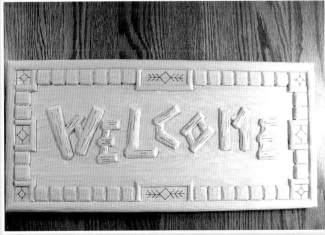

35 Transfer the patterns for the insets and the log detail.

36 Carve the inset designs using a detail knife and the same technique you used on the incised border of Block 1, Exercise 2 (see page 82). Use 1 mm V-tool to add line detail to the logs.

37 Set the finished sign aside as you make the cutouts.

38 Carve off the sawed edges of each cutout (tree, bear, moose, and fish). The grain of the wood should run from the top to the bottom on the tree, the bear, and the moose. The grain of the wood should run from the head to the tail on the fish.

39 Round the edges of each of the cutouts, and shave off the sawed edges on the front and back of each piece in the same fashion as the *Aztec Angels*, page 96. Be especially careful when working with the moose because his antlers are cross-grain and will break easily. Add the detail lines shown on the pattern templates for the ornaments using a 1 mm V-tool. The sign will be assembled after it is painted.

Attach the ornaments

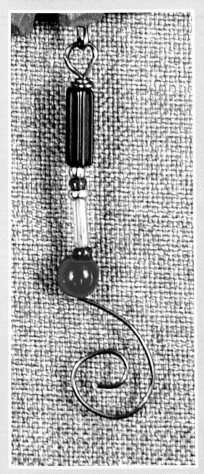

1. Using an 8" length of 22-gauge copper wire, fashion a spiral, as shown, for the lower bead strand.

2. String with a variety of beads to the desired length. Wrap the wire around a toothpick with needle-nose pliers to create a wire eye, and wrap the end back around the wire to secure. Cut off the remaining wire.

3. For the upper strand, make a wire eye on each end of the bead strand.

4. Make a wire staple by folding a short length of wire together, matching the ends. Slightly open the staple and insert it through the wire eye.

5. Using a manual drill and a ⅛" bit, carefully drill holes in the ornaments and on the lower edge of the *Welcome Sign* at the indicated points. Dry fit the ornament strands with staples in the holes. Cut the staple size down as required to fit.

6. Using instant glue, glue the ornament strands into their respective holes.

COLOR CHART

Maple Sugar Tan

Golden Brown

Hunter Green

Brown Iron Oxide

Western Sunset Yellow

Black Cherry

Barn Red

Antique with a combination of Spice Brown and Burnt Sienna.

More Great Project Books from Fox Chapel Publishing

Carving Santas from Around the World
15 Quick and Easy Projects to Make and Give
By Cyndi Joslyn

Learn to carve 15 festive and whimsical Santas with these easy-to-use plans. Includes helpful paint lists.

ISBN: 978-1-56523-187-0
$14.95 • 96 Pages

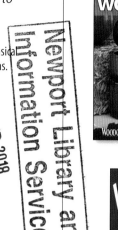

Halloween Woodcarving
Frightfully Fun Projects
By Cyndi Joslyn

Offering 10 original patterns and expert instructions to carve whimsical Halloween-inspired characters, including a mummy, witch, black cat, ghost, and more.

ISBN: 978-1-56523-289-1
$16.95 • 128 Pages

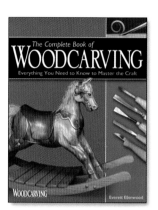

The Complete Book of Woodcarving
Everything You Need to Know to Master the Craft
By Everett Ellenwood

This comprehensive reference covers every classic style, along with power carving. Includes 9 projects and a helpful resource section.

ISBN: 978-1-56523-292-1
$27.95 • 288 Pages

The Little Book of Whittling
Passing Time on the Trail, on the Porch, and Under the Stars
By Chris Lubkemann

Learn to whittle a knife, spoon, goat head, canoe, and more. Makes a great gift.

ISBN: 978-1-56523-274-7
$12.95 • 104 Pages

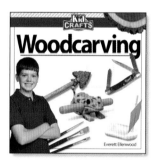

Kid Crafts Woodcarving
By Everett Ellenwood

Perfect for children or anyone learning to carve - includes basic carving skills and projects for a fun croaking frog, a snowman ornament, whistle, arrowhead, eagle's head, and more.

ISBN: 978-1-56523-366-9
$14.95 • 128 Pages

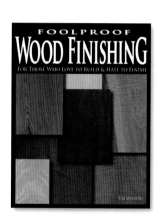

Foolproof Wood Finishing
The Complete Guide for Those Who Love to Build and Hate to Finish
By Teri Masaschi

Take the mystery out of finishing and avoid costly mistakes with easy-to-follow exercises designed by woodworking's premier finishing instructor.

ISBN: 978-1-56523-303-4
$19.95 • 200 Pages

WOODCARVING
ILLUSTRATED

In addition to being a leading source of woodworking books and DVDs, Fox Chapel also publishes *Woodcarving Illustrated*. Released quarterly, it delivers premium projects, expert tips and techniques from today's finest carvers, and in-depth information about the latest tools, equipment, & materials.

Subscribe Today!
Woodcarving Illustrated: **888-506-6630**
www.woodcarvingillustrated.com

Look For These Books at Your Local Bookstore or Woodworking Retailer
To order direct, call **800-457-9112** or visit *www.FoxChapelPublishing.com*

By mail, please send check or money order + $4.00 per book for S&H to: Fox Chapel Publishing, 1970 Broad Street, East Petersburg, PA 17520